Sandplay
Therapy
with
Children
and
Families

Sandplay Therapy with Children and Families

LOIS J. CAREY, M.S.W., B.C.D.S.W.

JASON ARONSON INC.
Northvale, New Jersey
London

This book was set in 11½ pt. Hiroshige Book by Alpha Graphics of Pittsfield, New Hampshire and printed and bound by Book-mart Press of North Bergen, New Jersey.

Library of Congress Cataloging-in-Publication Data

Carey, Lois J.
     Sandplay therapy with children and families / Lois J. Carey.
          p.   cm.
     Includes bibliographical references and index.
     ISBN 0-7657-0161-8
     1. Sandplay—Therapeutic use.   2. Family psychotherapy.   3. Child psychotherapy.   I. Title.
     RC489.S25C37   1998
     616.89'1653—dc21   97-50266

Printed in the United States of America on acid-free paper. Jason Aronson offers books and cassettes. For information and catalog write to Jason Aronson Inc., 230 Livingston Street, Northvale, New Jersey 07647-1726. Or visit our website: http://www.aronson.com

This book is lovingly dedicated to my husband, David;

my children and their spouses, David and Susan,

Norman and Nadine, Arlene and Bob;

to the future of the world, my grandchildren, Celia Keiser,

Dana Carey, Elena Carey, Robbie Keiser, and Doug Carey.

⟪ Contents ⟫

Foreword   ix
     Daniel S. Sweeney, Ph.D.

Preface   xxvii

1   Introduction to Individual Sandplay Therapy   1
2   Introduction to Sandplay Therapy
     with Families   31
3   Equipping and Maintaining a Sandplay Office   57
4   Beginning Treatment   67
5   Examples of Individual Sandplay Therapy   75
6   Examples of Family Sandplay Therapy   113
7   The Person of the Therapist   163
8   Similarities and Differences   173

Addendum: My Personal Journey   177

Appendix: Sample Permission Form and
     Suggested Miniatures and Sources   185

References   191

Credits   197

Index   199

ᨠ Foreword ᨦ

A young child walks into your office, hiding behind the legs of his parent. He is terrified. He has been sexually abused. You know that he needs to process the pain of his experience, and that the counseling process may be slow. He refuses to talk. Where do you begin? A family walks into your office, facing crisis, composed of parents who can't communicate and children responding by acting out. The system is crumbling, and at least some of them are asking for help. What do you do?

Many counselors might say these situations require that the clients *talk* about what has happened to them and what they are currently experiencing, that they must verbalize their frustration and pain as part of the healing process. My experience and the literature on play therapy and sandplay (Landreth et al. 1996), however, do not support this narrow conclusion.

Adult communication requires both verbal abilities and abstract thinking skills. A fundamental truth is that children do not communicate this way. Children communicate through play. Landreth (1991) suggested, "Children's play can be more fully appreciated when recognized as their natural medium of communication . . . for children to 'play out' their experiences and feelings is the most natural dynamic and self-healing process in which children can engage" (p. 10). Additionally, developmental psychology supports the use of play as a means for communicating with children. Play, like children, is pre-operational. Since children do not possess the developmental or intellectual sophistication to participate in adult verbally based therapies, it may be concluded that the very nature of childhood is fundamentally incompatible with the formal operations of adult counseling. To require a child to participate in adult therapy sends the message, "I am the expert. I expect you to come up to my level of communication. I am unwilling to enter your world."

I believe that these fundamental truths about how children communicate often apply to adults who have experienced conflict or trauma. In many ways, trauma (the severity of trauma covers a broad spectrum, and is therefore generally defined) is pre-operational. It impacts people of any age at a very basic and sensory level, and it does not lend itself to sophistication, categorization, or reason. To require a person of any age to verbalize when in an emotional crisis is not fair, and may in fact be retraumatizing. One way in which I illustrate this while conducting trainings on play therapy or sandplay is that I will often ask the audience for a volunteer to stand up and share with us his most embarrassing and traumatizing sexual experience. After the nervous laughter has subsided, I point out, "Isn't this what we do to child clients who have been molested whom we ask, 'Tell me what happened to you?'" (Sweeney 1997).

The very elemental and sensory aspects of trauma just noted indicate the need for a sensory-based treatment such as sandplay. Perhaps you have noticed that the diagnostic criteria for Posttraumatic Stress Disorder in the *DSM-IV* (1994) is largely sensory based. It recognizes that trauma itself is sensory based. In fact, many researchers believe that trauma memories are encoded not only in the brain but also within the body. It would seem, therefore, that a treatment approach for traumatized children, adults, and families should also be sensory based. Talk therapy approaches do not meet this criterion. Sandplay does.

In the next few pages, I'd like to talk about sand and play and therapy, and then discuss several rationales for using sandplay with children and families. Together with this book's author, I am convinced of the healing power of sandplay, and the efficacy of this important treatment modality.

SAND

Sand is the basic medium for this engrossing and effective treatment modality. It is a basic elemental compound, one of the most simple and common on earth. The choice to use sand as the foundation for sandplay was not accidental, but rather a natural phenomenon. The Old Testament tells us that "the Lord God formed man of the dust of the ground, and breathed into his nostrils the breath of life" (Genesis 2:7). Our connection to this earth is foundational. This is not accidental, but rather providential design. As we connect with the sand, we cannot help but feel the connection to the spirit within and the Creation without.

Sand is also a reminder of history. A single grain of sand may have traveled thousands of miles and an equal number of years before coming to its current place of rest. Geology reminds us that a "grain was produced by forces that made the rock it was eroded from, by the Earth's surface environment that eroded it from its parent and carried it to a resting place, and by the internal deformation of the Earth's crust that buried it" (Siever 1988, p. 1). People have had much the same experience. Many forces have come to bear on every person: some from the family of origin, some from other socioenvironmental factors, and some from crisis and trauma. The "internal deformation" of a grain of sand speaks metaphorically of the intrapsychic pain that many of our clients bring to us. Sand is a product of its history, and so are we.

While many factors are involved, it is because of this—this core, this essence, and this foundational element of sand—that sandplay can be so impacting. Therapeutic connection and the processing of rooted emotional turmoil are not merely assisted by the use of sand. It is the sand that creates the path. Eichoff (1952) suggested that sand was the "means of which gross feelings can be expressed, for it can be thrown, tossed, molded, plastered, dug and smoothed; and on this base concrete symbols can be placed . . ." (p. 235). Sand is more than a therapeutic medium. It is a means of expressing the very core of who we are. Indeed, as Dora Kalff (1980) so succinctly stated, "The act of playing in the sand allows the patient to come near his own totality" (p. vii).

PLAY AND THERAPY

Like sand, play, in and of itself, is therapeutic. This is an accepted maxim for the sandplay therapist, and a wonderful discovery for the sandplay client. Caplan and Caplan (1974) proposed several unique attributes about the process of play: (1) play is voluntary by nature and, in a world full of rules and requirements, play is refreshing and full of respite; (2) play is free from evaluation and judgment; thus it is safe to make mistakes without failure; (3) play encourages fantasy and the use of the imagination, enabling control without competition; (4) play increases involvement and interest; and (5) play encourages the development of self.

The marriage of a therapeutic activity with the process of psychotherapy is a natural evolution. Play therapy, in all of its expressions, has increased in its utilization, and has demonstrated its efficacy (Landreth et al. 1996). It becomes important, therefore, to bring some definition to the process.

Play therapy involves more than the application of traditional talk therapy accompanied by some type of play media. According to Landreth (1991), play therapy is defined as "a dynamic interpersonal relationship between a child and a therapist trained in play therapy procedures who provides selected play materials and facilitates the development of a safe relationship for the child to fully express and explore self (feelings, thoughts, experiences, and behaviors) through the child's natural medium of communication, play" (p. 14). This is a comprehensive definition that applies to the world of sandplay as well.

Sandplay should involve a *dynamic interpersonal relationship*. Regardless of the specific therapeutic and theoretical approach one takes to the sandplay process, the evolution and development of a dynamic interpersonal relationship is crucial. Kalff (1980) stressed the importance of the therapist creating a "free and protected space," noting that it is the love of the therapist that creates this space. The sandplay therapist should be *trained in (sand)play therapy procedures*. Appropriate training and supervised experience, as well as personal sandplay exposure, is crucial for the therapist interested in doing sandplay. The ethical and responsible psychotherapist will become theoretically and practically grounded in any modality before its employment. This is particularly important in sandplay. As with any play therapy modality it is crucial to *provide selected play materials* in the sandplay process, as will be described later in this book. A random collection of sandplay miniatures is not appropriate; an intentional and deliberate selection is. A client may be confused by a disorganized collection, emotionally flooded by an unlimited collection, or confined by a limited collection. This should be a natural outgrowth of the sandplay therapist's training and evolving experience.

The sandplay therapist should *facilitate*, rather than direct, the therapeutic experience. Children and families enter into the therapy process already feeling disempowered and out of control. As the sandplay therapist facilitates rather than choreographs the process, clients will experience healing through a growing sense of self-control, empowerment, and safety. Siegelman (1990) described this facilitation process well: "To be a participant–observer at the moment when a frightened or constricted patient feels securely enough held to take her first step into the realm of symbolic play—this is being a midwife to the birth of the capacity for meaning" (p. 175). This facilitation creates the opportunity for the client to *fully express and explore self*. Self-expression and self-exploration are crucial in the counseling process, and are foundational in sandplay. Kalff (1981) stressed this exploration of self: "the patient, through the sandplay, penetrates to that which we can recognize as an expression of Self" (p. viii).

Finally, the last element of Landreth's definition particularly applies to the sandplay process. Play is more than just a child's *natural medium of communication*. As suggested above, I would assert that the natural medium of communication for the client in crisis involves some type of expressive medium.

Play therapy and sandplay are often thought to be treatment modalities for the individual. I share the enthusiasm with this book's author, however, that sandplay with families is exciting and effective. The marriage of family therapy and sandplay is a natural union. Eliana Gil (1994) posited, "Family therapists and play therapists share a noble trait: They are by far the most creative and dynamic therapists in existence. Family therapists . . . engage the family's participation in a dynamic way, either by intensifying or replacing verbal communication" (p. 34).

Family therapy that does not actively and intentionally provide means to include children, such as an expressive media like sandplay, is not truly *family* therapy. While a systemic approach to treating families is frequently preached and lauded, the exclusion of children from the process barely makes the treatment systemic. Nathan Ackerman (1970), one of the pioneers in the field, wrote that "without engaging the children in a meaningful interchange across the generations, there can be no family therapy" (p. 403). Sandplay creates a bridge for meaningful interchanges to take place. The content of sandplay provides a metaphorical blueprint of family alliances, personality stages, and intergenerational patterns. As a largely undefended mode of expression, sandplay, like art therapy, provides the therapist with the opportunity to access information that might not be verbally disclosed, as well as the opportunity to observe the family's emotional climate (Kwiatkowska 1978).

SANDPLAY: BENEFITS AND RATIONALE

Children and families yearn for a place in which to express and process their pain. For many of them, the prospect of psychotherapy is enormously daunting. To verbalize issues means to confront fearful emotions. Even the most cooperative client must deal with the difficulties this confrontation presents. Sandplay provides a safe place for this often intimidating process to occur. I am convinced not only of its efficacy as a treatment, but of its quality as a place of retreat for the client in pain. I would like to list several rationales, as well as practical benefits, for the use of sandplay with children and families. These are not listed in any priority.

1. Sandplay Gives Expression to Nonverbalized Emotional Issues

Since play is the language of childhood, as well as a language for a client of any age who is unable or unwilling to verbalize, the sand tray provides a safe medium for expression. If play is the language, then the miniatures are the words. Just as an empty canvas provides a place for the artist's expression, so the tray provides a place for the client's emotional expression. The client needs no creative or artistic ability since the medium provides a flow void of evaluation.

The self-directed sandplay process allows clients to be fully themselves. Through the process of sandplay, which includes a caring and accepting relationship, children and families can express their total personalities. This enables clients in distress to consider new possibilities, some of which are not possible through verbal expression, and thus to significantly develop the expression of self. Sandplay is, therefore, more than a symbolization of the psyche—it is a forum for full self-expression and self-exploration.

2. Sandplay Has a Unique Kinesthetic Quality

I have already reflected on the sensory quality of sand and play, and the need for a sensory experience for clients in crisis. Sandplay provides this sensory experience, and meets the need that we all have for kinesthetic experiences. This fundamental essential, an extension of very basic attachment needs, is met through relationship and experience. Sandplay provides both of these elements for clients.

The very tactile experience of touching and manipulating the sand is a therapeutic experience in and of itself. I have frequently had nonverbal clients who have done nothing more than run their fingers through the sand and then begin to talk about deep issues, as if the sensory experience with the sand causes a loosening of the tongue. While this has not been my intent or my goal, it is certainly a therapeutic by-product. The manipulation of the sand and placement of the miniatures is both safe and kinesthetically satisfying, especially for clients whose prior sensory experience was noxious.

3. Sandplay Serves to Create a Therapeutic Distance for Clients

The child client or family in emotional crisis is often unable to express pain in words, but may find expression through a projective medium such as sandplay. It is simply easier for a traumatized client to "speak" through one of the sandplay miniatures than to verbalize the pain. The consistency of the medium and the consistency of the therapist in allowing the client to direct the process creates a place where the degree of therapeutic distance is set by the client. Children and families in sandplay may experience emotional release through symbolization and sublimation, through the projection onto the tray and miniatures.

4. The Therapeutic Distance That Sandplay Provides Creates a Safe Place for Abreaction to Occur

Children and families that have experienced trauma need a therapeutic setting in which to abreact, a place where repressed issues can emerge and be relived and where the negative emotions that are frequently attached can be experienced. Abreaction, a crucial element in the treatment of trauma, finds facilitated expression.

Schaefer (1994) suggested several properties that provide the sense of distance and safety that reluctant children in families gain in sandplay: (1) symbolization: children can use a predatory miniature to represent an abuser; (2) "as if" quality: children can use the pretend quality of sandplay to act out events as if they are not real life; (3) projection: children can project intense emotions onto the miniatures, which can then safely act out these feelings; and (4) displacement: children can displace negative feelings onto the miniatures rather than expressing them toward family members. Sandplay provides not only the opportunity for abreaction to occur, but facilitates the process through the setting and media.

5. *Sandplay with Families Is a Truly Inclusive Experience*

As noted, an adult talk therapy approach to treating families is decidedly exclusive, as it fails to recognize and honor the developmental level of children in the family. Sandplay with families overcomes this obstacle. Sandplay creates a level playing field for every family member, giving all of them the opportunity to express themselves. Keith and Whitaker (1981) include play therapy interventions as an integral part of the family treatment process, concluding that "fundamental family therapy takes place at this nonverbal level" (p. 249).

For example, it can be very threatening to ask a child to detail the communication patterns in the family through words. It can be equally threatening for any member of the family who feels isolated or disempowered. Put simply, it is not okay to "air the dirty laundry," especially to an outsider. Family members shouldn't talk about problems—perhaps the sandplay miniatures can! The typical family sculpting exercise, which can be overwhelming for children to do in a family session, may easily be replicated in the sand tray. Like puppet play, sandplay can create "an unrealistic and nonthreatening atmosphere that assists in the identification process, thereby encouraging the projection of emotional aspects and interpersonal relationships through the characters" (Bow 1993, p. 28).

6. *Sandplay Naturally Provides Boundaries and Limits, Which Promote Safety for the Client*

The therapeutic relationship, as well as any other relationship, is defined by boundaries and limits. Sweeney (1997) suggested

"A relationship without boundaries is not a relationship; rather, it is an unstructured attempt at connection that cannot be made because the people have no specific rules for engagement. A world without limits is not a safe world, and children do not grow where they do not feel safe" (p. 103).

The careful structure of the sandplay process and the carefully selected tools of the sandplay therapist provide the client with the boundaries that create the sense of safety needed for growth. The size of the sand tray, the size and selection of miniatures, the office setting, and the guidance and instruction of the therapist all provide boundaries and limits for the client. While these limits are imperative and intentional, they promote freedom for expression. These inherent limits to sandplay bring focus to the therapeutic process that, in addition to promoting the safety that boundaries bring, assists the client to focus on the therapeutic issues to be addressed.

7. Sandplay Provides a Unique Setting for the Emergence of Therapeutic Metaphors

There is an increasing amount of literature on metaphors and psychotherapy, much of which focuses on verbal metaphors. Siegelman (1990) suggested that metaphors "combine the abstract and the concrete in a special way, enabling us to go from the known and the sensed to the unknown, and the symbolic. . . . They achieve this combination in a way that typically arises from and produces strong feeling that leads to integrating insight" (p. ix). Metaphors can indeed be therapeutically powerful. I would suggest that the most powerful metaphors in therapy are those that are generated by the clients themselves.

Sandplay creates a consummate setting for this to occur. The sand and miniatures are ideal for clients to express their own therapeutic metaphors.

Where therapeutic metaphors emerge, there naturally follows a therapeutic interpretation. I would echo Kalff's (1980) warning against focusing on interpretation, recognizing that it is the client's interpretation that is the most important. I would further suggest that interpretation of sand trays is not essential to the healing process, and often need to remind myself that, when I interpret, I do so with my own mind and experience, not the client's. It is a helpful reminder that when interpreting a client's expression of an experience, the sharing of the interpretation is meant to serve the client's need and not the therapist's.

8. *Sandplay Is Effective in Overcoming Client Resistance*

It is important to remember when working with children and families that involuntary clients are the rule of thumb. Children generally do not self-refer, and not all family members are enthusiastic about entering therapy. Sandplay, because of its nonthreatening and engaging qualities, can captivate the involuntary client and draw in the reticent family member. Since play is the natural medium of communication for children, the child client who has been compelled into therapy by an adult is generally amenable to treatment because she is being allowed to express self through play.

For the resistant family member, sandplay provides a means of communicating that diverts the fear of verbal conflict. The level of contribution that each family member brings to the construction of the sand tray may be a reflection of his or her investment in family. In this regard, resistance can not only be overcome by sandplay but can be more fully identified as well.

9. Sandplay Provides a Needed and Effective Communication Medium for the Client with Poor Verbal Skills

Beyond the developmental importance of providing children with a nonverbal therapeutic medium, there are clients of all ages who have poor verbal skills for a variety of reasons. These include clients who experience developmental language delays or deficits, clients with social or relational difficulties, clients with physiological challenges, and more.

Like the toddler who wants something desperately but cannot communicate this to the parent, anyone unable to effectively communicate his needs can experience great frustration. When the toddler has a tantrum because he cannot communicate his wants or needs, there is a vivid relationship challenge between parent and child. In the same way, relationship challenges of many types emerge in families when people are not able to verbalize their wants and needs. The sandplay process creates a place where expression of needs and wants is not dependent on words. The client with poor verbal skills, regardless of the etiology, finds a place of relief in sandplay—a place where expression does not depend on verbal acuity, but occurs through the freedom of the medium.

10. Sandplay Cuts Through
Verbalization Used as a Defense

For the pseudomature child who presents as verbally astute yet is developmentally unable to effectively communicate on a cognitive level, sandplay provides a means to communicate through the child's true and natural medium of communication. For the verbally sophisticated adult who uses intellectualization and rationalization as a defense, sandplay may cut through these defenses. This is an important dynamic to be aware of, since a family system that includes a verbally well-defended member also includes one or more members unable to establish effective communication and relationship. The nonverbal and expressive nature of sandplay identifies this dynamic and provides a nonverbal way to address it.

11. Sandplay Creates a Place for the
Child Client or Family to Experience Control

One of the primary results of crisis and trauma is a loss of control for people in its midst. The loss of emotional, psychological, and even physiological control is one of the most distressing byproducts of crisis and conflict. Both the individual and family in crisis feel the frustration and fear of having lost control. A crucial goal for these clients must be to empower them, following any personal or family trauma that has been disempowering.

The self-directed process of sandplay creates a place for control to be returned to the client. For the client looking to attain and extend self-control, sandplay establishes the boundaries and allows the freedom for this to occur. For the client attempting to avoid responsibility, the sandplay process places the responsibility for and control of the process on the client. If a goal of therapy is to help clients achieve a greater internal locus of control, sandplay is an effective means toward this end.

12. *The Challenge of Transference May Be Effectively Addressed through Sandplay*

The presence of an expressive medium creates an alternative object of transference. Lowenfeld (1979) proposed that in the creation of worlds in the sand, any transference occurs between the client and the tray, rather than between the client and the therapist. Weinrib (1983) noted that the sand tray often becomes an independent object, so that the client may take away images of the tray rather than the therapist. Regardless of one's theoretical view of transference, however, sandplay provides a means for transference issues to be safely addressed as needed. The tray and miniatures may become objects of transference or the means by which transference issues are safely addressed.

13. *Deeper Intrapsychic Issues May Be Accessed More Thoroughly and More Rapidly through Sandplay*

Access to underlying emotional issues and unconscious conflicts is a challenge for any counselor. Although certainly not a comprehensive list, the qualities of sandplay that have been suggested above generate an atmosphere where deep and complex intrapsychic issues can be safely approached.

Most clients have some level of motivation to change, as reflected by their presence in psychotherapy. Most of these clients likewise are often well defended when confronting challenges to their ego, which has already been injured. Sandplay serves to decrease ego controls and other defenses and to foster greater levels of disclosure. This in turn creates an increased capacity to consider interpersonal and intrapersonal alternatives.

CONCLUSION

There are a myriad of techniques used and advocated in the mental health profession. People in pain, however, are not healed through technique. People experience emotional healing when they encounter someone and when they encounter self. It is an inner process, a relational process, and a heart process. To once again refer to the Old Testament, we are told, "Keep thy heart with all diligence; for out of it are the issues of life" (Proverbs 4:23). Verbal therapies that keep the focus on cognitive issues don't consider the importance of the heart, which brings to us the issues of life. I submit that sandplay is more than just another treatment modality, because sandplay seeks and maintains this inner core. Spare (1981) wrote, "As with every aspect of clinical practice, meaningful use of sandplay is a function of our own human hearts, and of the ever ongoing interplay between our own centers and the centers, hearts, and needs of those we are privileged to see in psychotherapy" (p. 208).

Sandplay has enjoyed increasing popularity among psychotherapists seeking expressive interventions with their clients. As earlier suggested, this popularity, however, has not always been accompanied by adequate training and experience. The interested reader who is a novice to the field is encouraged to seek adequate training, supervised experience, and personal sandplay therapy. The more experienced sandplay therapist is encouraged to glean some of the valuable nuggets of information in this book so that new things may be incorporated with clients and new ideas stimulated. Sandplay is so much more than a mere treatment modality. It is a path for the hurting to heal and the healthy to grow. The road of counseling needs to see more footprints in this sandy path.

Daniel S. Sweeney, Ph.D.

✍ Preface ✍

This book has presented a challenge far beyond what I anticipated when I began writing it some months ago. I was ill prepared for the extensive validation of sources that is needed to produce such a complex work, or for the uncounted hours of thought, planning, execution, writing, and rewriting that are involved. Since I have been engaged in sandplay work for a number of years, I expected that a book would flow naturally. However, every task, whether we anticipate it or not, offers a learning experience. This has certainly been the case for me. Much of the content of this book has been taken from personal notes that have been gleaned over the years from my attendance at Sandplay and other Jungian conferences and workshops, as well as from my involvement in family therapy. It is impossible to document all of the sources in those instances.

The melding of family therapy and Jungian Sandplay has been accomplished largely through my own pioneering effort. I believe that my article, "Family Sandplay Therapy" (1991), was one of the first such attempts to combine these two modalities. I am aware that those therapists who practice from a Jungian orientation might dispute the use of sandplay with families, but I am convinced that this combination of modalities has a place in the therapeutic armamentarium.

For the purpose of clarification, individual Jungian Sand-play will be referred to in this book with a capital "S," family systems and other orientations to sandplay with a small "s." I have chosen to use either "he" or "she" terminology throughout most of this book to designate gender references (for patients and/or therapists) rather than the more awkward "he/she" and ask the reader's indulgence with respect to this issue. In those instances where the gender is case-specific, I have used the appropriate term.

My introduction and interest in things Jungian evolved from my own personal analysis. I am not a certified Jungian analyst; however, the main thrust of my work is based on theories that were developed by Jung and his followers, and on which I have spent many years of study.

My interest in family therapy grew out of my social work training at Columbia University and additional training in family therapy, which has included numerous workshops and conferences.

Work with children, especially children who have experienced loss, grew out of my own history. I was a "child of divorce," long before anyone understood the significance of that term.

I would like to give special thanks to the following persons who have been so influential in supporting my efforts. These are listed in no particular order: Ron Grant, Edith Sullwold, Dora Kalff, Louise Mahdi, Brewster Beach, John Johnson, Geneviève Geer, Edith Wallace, Charles Schaefer, John Allan, Garry Landreth, Nancy Barrett, Sidney Mackenzie, Helen Linder, Emily Marlin, and Nancy Boyd-Webb.

I also want to thank the many organizations here and abroad that have invited me to speak to them on topics related to both Jungian Sandplay and sandplay with families. A special thanks also to families who have permitted use of their and their children's case material and photographs.

Lynn Temple, a very talented friend, deserves a special thank you for her untiring editorial help; Daniel Sweeney's thoughtful writing of the Foreword is very gratefully acknowleged as well; and thanks also to Charles Schaefer, and Jason Aronson and his staff for giving me the opportunity to publish this book.

These notes of thanks would not be complete without mentioning my family (the family of origin as well as the nuclear one), from whom I have learned more than they could ever guess.

‹‹◎ 1 ◎››

Introduction to Individual Sandplay Therapy

The psychotherapeutic technique known as Sandplay has experienced a major growth in popularity within the past five to ten years, as witnessed by the publication of numerous articles and several books devoted to this topic. Sandplay has been enthusiastically adopted by play therapists and art therapists, as well as by Jungian psychotherapists in their search for creative ways to assist young patients and their families.

Sandplay therapy is an exciting, challenging prospect for any practitioner who might want to add it to her practice, one that warrants close examination. It is a very powerful technique that needs to be thoroughly understood, solidly grounded in theory, and carefully implemented in order to provide the most positive therapeutic outcome for the patient. There are many therapists today with no basic training or personal experience with this medium who have nonetheless begun to use sandplay. Such a person is like an untrained practitioner using art therapy: while anyone can encourage a patient to draw something, if the therapist has no understanding of the significance of line, color, placement on the page, relative size, pencil pressure, and so on, the work that is produced will have little therapeutic value. In addition to a lack of training, many therapists who undertake to use this powerful tool have unfortunately had no experience with the process themselves. Both a sound theoretical foundation and some active personal involvement in Sandplay are essential if one is to reap the full benefits of this medium.

Today, sandplay therapists come from a wide range of theoretical orientations. The Jungian archetypal model, because it played so pivotal a role historically, will provide the main theoretical foundation for the present discussion.

Sandplay as practiced today was first developed by Dora Kalff, a Swiss Jungian analyst, who based her work upon Margaret Lowenfeld's World Technique and then combined it with the theories of Carl Jung. For this reason, Sandplay has been heavily influenced by the Lowenfeld and Jung approaches, to which Frau Kalff added her interest in Zen Buddhism as well as her own creative talents. Lowenfeld (1979) wrote: "Toys to children are like culinary implements to the kitchen; every kitchen has them and has also the elements of food. It is what the cook does with the implements and elements that determines the dish" (p. 3).

This book is designed to offer two diverse methods for combining the elements that can be effectively utilized with Sandplay. It will offer a theoretical background for a Jungian approach with an individual child and it will also offer a family systems orientation that is often useful when one opts to include a child-centered family approach in play therapy.

PIONEERS

Navajo Indians

The Navajo Indian rites of healing have been cited as indirect contributors to the understanding of Sandplay. This is well described by Estelle Weinrib in her book *Images of the Self* (1983). The procedure consists of the medicine man drawing a picture in the sand depicting symbolic scenes. These are generally in a round, or mandala, shape. The ill or traumatized person sits in the center of the mandala and the medicine man chants healing invocations in order to drive the devils out of him. One side of the mandala is always left open so the evil can escape from the patient. The Navajo people believe that sand itself has the capacity to draw evil spirits from the afflicted while, at the same time, providing him with good spirits.

Margaret Lowenfeld

Sandplay as a therapeutic modality has been in existence since 1929, when Margaret Lowenfeld first devised a method known as the World Technique. Dr. Lowenfeld was a child psychiatrist in London, where she established the Institute for Child Psychology. Her influence was felt by many clinicians, and the technique took different forms as her trainees adapted their methods to their own theoretical orientations. Lowenfeld writes (1979):

> A psychoanalyst will find sexual themes, sometimes symbolically represented there, for the reason that sexuality does play a part in a child's "World" picture. The Adlerian will undoubtedly find the power complex. . . . The "World" apparatus should

appeal to the heart of the Jungian, seeing that the "World" cabinet is richly furnished with already completed archetypal symbols. [p. 7]

Since this book encompasses not only Jungian Sandplay but also family sandplay, it is important to note that family systems practitioners look at these "Worlds" through the lens of family interactions (see Chapters Two and Six).

In the comprehensive study published by Rie Rogers Mitchell and Harriet Friedman (1994), Lowenfeld's influence is described as quite far-reaching. Many of the practitioners who met with Lowenfeld adapted their own orientations to her teachings. Erik Erikson, Gudrun Seitz in Sweden, and Dora Kalff in Switzerland were among those whom Lowenfeld influenced.

Lowenfeld had an interesting history. She was born in England and spent her early years in both Poland and England. Her father was Polish and had become successful in business dealings. Margaret had one older sister who was quite gifted and successful. Margaret, on the other hand, "described herself as an unhappy and delicate child. She spent a large part of her childhood ill in bed, enduring long periods of solitude" (Mitchell and Friedman 1994, p. 5).

When Margaret was 13, her parents divorced, causing her a great deal of anguish. She and her sister remained with their mother, who had progressive ideas regarding her daughters' education, in contrast to the views held by their father. He believed they should become traditional young Englishwomen and devote themselves to home and family. Both sisters, however, became physicians.

Because of her early childhood experiences with illness and divorce, Lowenfeld sensed intuitively that children often did not possess the necessary language to convey their deepest feelings. For this reason she sought, through her work, to find methods that would enable a child to *show* her, rather than *tell* her, what the problem was.

Lowenfeld herself did not take credit for the initial development of sandplay into a therapeutic technique. Instead, she said that it was the children who developed the process while she only provided a sand box and toys for them to use. She described herself as the observer who took note of what the children produced in the sand, then asked them to tell her about the scene.

In addition to Lowenfeld's major studies on the child's use of sand and miniatures, she also developed another diagnostic instrument, known as the Mosaic Test. This test involves the construction of a picture using plastic tiles of different shapes, sizes, and colors. When Lowenfeld analyzed these mosaics and then compared them to a child's sand World constructions, she was able to clearly conceptualize a child's inner state.

Lowenfeld was also quite interested in the arts and literature, and compared some of the ideas from the arts to themes she had observed in a child's therapy, especially Chagall's technique in which different images are contained within a single larger image. Her concept of *clusters* grew out of this observation (Lowenfeld 1979). She illustrates how several experiences of a child can be superimposed upon each other, causing an emotional reaction. One example might be a child who, at one period of life, suffers from a serious asthma attack that ends in hospitalization and, at a later period, is attacked by a vicious dog. Each of these incidents causes panic reactions for the child. Later, through "sand/world play," both experiences might be depicted in disguised form. She referred to this process (showing two or three traumatic incidents at the same time) as *clusters*. Lowenfeld also disagreed with the Freudian concepts of conscious and unconscious, instead positing that there were two separate systems in operation: Primary and Secondary. The *Primary* system is what is most directly linked to the unconscious process, especially as experienced prior to language development. The *Secondary* system is the more conscious aspect, when language and thought can be expressed. Lowenfeld believed that the combination of Primary and Secondary processes was what gave each individual his own uniqueness.

Lowenfeld (1979) asserts that "the qualities of the World apparatus from which its power of expression derives" are its "multi-dimensional nature, the dynamic possibilities it offers, the power of the apparatus to present states of mind hitherto unknown, and its independence of skill" (pp. 13–14).

In order to assess Lowenfeld's work, Ruth Bowyer (1970), Charlotte Buhler (1951a,b, 1952), and Liselotte Fischer (1950) all studied and verified her findings through experimental research. Their research is of special interest in documenting the types of cases suitable for therapy through use of the World Technique, and is well described by Mitchell and Friedman (1994).

Charlotte Buhler recognized the potential of using miniatures as a diagnostic and research instrument. She created the World Test (1951a), which was later called the Toy World Test, in order to differentiate it from Lowenfeld's World Technique. As part of Buhler's research (1952), she also compared children from various cultures and found that their cultural backgrounds were reflected in what they produced.

Lowenfeld found that emotionally disturbed children often fenced in large parts of the World, or placed wild animals where they did not belong, or placed objects in unusual surroundings. They also used the same objects repeatedly. These observations of Lowenfeld were confirmed by Buhler's studies (1951a,b, Buhler and Kelly 1941).

Buhler identified three signs which she felt had relevance to the World Test. These were defined in a monograph (1951b) and are summarized below.

1. A-signs—Aggressive World Signs

These were indicated by soldiers fighting, animals biting, or other forms of aggression. She found some aggression to be normal in children, most often manifested in creations that followed the construction of the initial sand world. When A-signs were seen in the *initial* tray this suggested to her the possibility of a more intense aggressiveness than is usual. She also found that accidents were depicted more frequently in the sand trays of children who were disturbed, and when a number of accidents were portrayed it suggested to her the need for therapy. There were times, however, when instruments of aggression could be seen in the positive role of protection and defense.

2. E-signs—Empty World Signs

These occurred when there were fewer than fifty toys used, when the toys that were selected came from only a few categories, when major groups of people were omitted (e.g., no adults, or only children, or only soldiers and police). Buhler said that the sand tray worlds of children under 8 are normally quite empty. The empty world suggested to her an interior emptiness, or feelings of loneliness, or a need to be alone. E-signs could also suggest resistance to the task, an emotional fixation on certain objects, or blocked creativity. Complete omission of people could have a double meaning: either the desire to escape from people or else to defy them.

There could be disagreement with Buhler's observations that these worlds of children under 8 are normally quite empty. Many younger children use numerous items somewhat randomly and only later in therapy do they become more selective in portraying their inner situations.

3. CRD-signs—Closed, Rigid and
   Disorganized Worlds

This type of world is partially or completely fenced in, there are unrealistic rows of animals, people, or things lined up in a fixed, stiff manner, or there are disorganized worlds in chaotic form. Buhler noted that CRD-signs were more significant symptoms of emotional disturbance than either of the other two types. CRD-signs could also indicate an unusual need for security or protection. They might also signal rigidity or confusion. If a client set up fences before any other materials were used, it indicated to her an unusual need for protection. This phenomenon has been observed in initial sessions with some highly anxious children. Rigid worlds can also indicate varying degrees of compulsive orderliness, perfectionism, and excessive fear.

Disorganized worlds did not necessarily indicate deep emotional disturbance for young children but, for older children or adults, they could indicate varying degrees of confusion and dissolution of the personality structure. Buhler did not indicate what ages she was referring to when she spoke of young children.

As part of Buhler's studies, she found that retarded individuals had significantly more empty and distorted worlds than others. She also noted that in some cases the memory of a traumatic experience, triggered by the handling of the miniatures, could be so overwhelming that no construction at all took place.

Laura Ruth Bowyer (1970) was another researcher of the Lowenfeld technique. Her studies confirmed those of Buhler and incorporated the developmental stages of the child to the overall evaluation of the Worlds. For example, it is common for a young child of 2 or 3 to engage in burying toys and then finding them in the sand, which symbolically represents the child's search for object constancy. When this activity is performed by a child of 8 or 9, it can be interpreted as a regression to an earlier stage of development.

These early researchers explored the relationship between child developmental stages and stages of development as they were revealed in sand productions. They hoped to learn if there were common threads among different age groups and studied themes that were common to various age groups in order to distinguish the "normal" from the "pathological." This work continues today, as there is a continuing need for refining the standardization and verification of norms in Sandplay.

Margareta Sjolund (1981), writing about child therapy in Sweden, states that in the 1940s play materials were used as diagnostic indicators at the Erica Institute in Stockholm. This Institute was founded by Gosta Harding. The Erica Method is a more structured approach than that used by either the Lowenfeld or Kalff practitioners and it is not too widely known in the United States. An identical set of 360 toys is used by each Erica practitioner. The toys have a uniform shape and are similar in size.

In the Jungian and Lowenfeldian approaches, each therapist is free to select the miniatures that seem to hold the most meaning for him as well as for his clients. Dora Kalff, in a training session (1980), said there should be nothing in a therapist's collection that the therapist cannot relate to, because then it would have no personal meaning. For example, a therapist might have one interpretation for a figure while the patient has a totally different one. By incorporating both interpretations into understanding a symbol, the work is broadened and enriched.

It has been said that "there on the shelves of each Sandplay therapist sits the unconscious of the therapist for all to see." Each Sandplay office has its own unique arrangement and reflects the choices made by the therapist. Because of this, I believe it might be extremely difficult, if not impossible, for two therapists to share a Sandplay office.

CARL JUNG

Jung's influence in Sandplay is very significant. Dr. Jung is credited with an early form of play therapy, which is described in his autobiography *Memories, Dreams, Reflections* (1965). Following his break from Freud, Jung attempted to integrate this devastating experience and found that play techniques were extremely useful. He kept thinking about how he had played as a child, and of the comfort he had received from this play. He realized that he needed to find a way back to this period of his life for any resolution of his conflict to occur. So in 1912, Jung began to construct a miniature village that he made from rocks and stones that he gathered from the lake shore at his summer home in Bollingen. This activity led him to a stream of fantasies, which he later wrote down. The experience was a direct contribution to his work on active imagination, as well as to other theories that he was in the process of developing.

Especially relevant to the work of Sandplay is Jung's description of the archetype of the child (1959).

> The "child" is all that is abandoned and exposed and at the same time divinely powerful; the insignificant, dubious beginning, and the triumphal end. The "eternal child" in man is an indescribable experience, an incongruity, a handicap, and a divine prerogative; an imponderable that determines the ultimate worth or worthlessness of a personality. [p. 179]

At an international psychoanalytic conference in 1937, Jung heard Dr. Lowenfeld lecture on the World Technique. He was struck by the similarities to the experience he had had of building his miniature village. Jung was quite impressed by Lowenfeld's presentation, especially since he could see the possibility of contacting the archetypal level of the psyche in this way. This insight was incorporated some time later, through the work of Frau Kalff.

Jung's archetypal theories are what differentiate this method from other applications of sandplay. The ability to understand the archetypal level of the psyche through Jungian Sandplay enables deeper healing to occur than is possible when other theoretical bases are employed. This is not meant to imply that other theories do not have their place in treatment. It does suggest, however, that there is the possibility of reaching the soul-level through contacting and mediating with the archetypes. Marion Woodman (1993), Canadian Jungian analyst, says, "Psychological work is soul work. Psychology is the science of the soul. By soul, I mean the eternal part of ourselves that wants to create timeless objects like art" (p. 3).

Jung spent many years in his research on the archetypal level of the psyche, and this was one of the main reasons for his break with Freud. Jung had a dream that he related to Freud, who analyzed it in a reductionistic fashion, but that Jung knew had far greater significance. The dream was quite lengthy, but the theme was that Jung was in a house he was not familiar with and, as he went down from one floor to the floor below, he found that with each descent to a lower level the lighting became dimmer and dimmer. As he continued to go down, he found that the artifacts on each level became more and more ancient, going from modern to very primitive (Jung 1965). Jung compared the house to the psyche and believed that the deeper one proceeded through the various layers, the more likely it was that one could contact the deep archetypal level. He believed that it was only through exploring this archetypal level that deep healing could occur. For the reader with a limited knowledge of archetypes, I am including the following section. Interested persons are directed to the references for a more in-depth analysis of archetypes.

Archetypes

Wilmer (1991) writes,

the world of the archetypes is that invisible world that no one has ever seen. It is hypothesized to be the deepest realm of the psyche and to have the potential to evoke images of a more or less predictable nature. It is these images that we see and which occur worldwide in the psyches of all people. The same images have been appearing and reappearing from time immemorial. We know them through fairy tales, sagas, legends, and stories told the world over. They transcend culture, race and time. [p. 56]

An archetype is nothing more or less than a hypothetical model that is never fully or finally explained. We can only approximate the meaning of any particular archetype, as each person experiences it in his or her own particular way. Everyone, for example, would have a different internal image of what is meant by *mother* or *father, horse* or *dragon.*

A most important aspect of any single archetype is that it is two-sided and has both positive and negative poles. When emotional problems arise, they are often due to the existence of an archetypal imbalance. The negative pole is the one that seems to cause the most psychological suffering; however, too much of the positive can be equally problematic. The main thrust of all archetypal understanding is the need to attain a balance between these positive and negative aspects in order to be as individuated as possible. *Individuation,* to use Jung's term, is the balance that is sought through mediating with the archetypes. It is a process of archetypal actualization. It is possible to contact and mediate with these archetypal images through dreams, art work, writing, or Sandplay. Every major theorist has concluded that this is a lifelong task, one that is never fully attained, as there is always more one can learn about oneself.

Jungian therapists seek to locate the connections between the conscious mind of the patient and the unconscious archetypes that are the cause of personal suffering. The problem that arises when archetypes remain solely in the unconscious is that the patient can become *identified* with an archetype, which can cause many problems. This is often referred to as a *complex*. A complex, as such, is normal, but it can become pathological when one is in the grip of an archetype.

The *Great Mother* is probably the most commonly seen and most troublesome. As with all archetypes, she takes both positive and negative forms and can lead to a *Mother Complex*. (*The Great Mother: An Analysis of the Archetype* (1972), by Erich Neumann, is a classic work.) On its positive side, this archetype can be nurturing, all-giving, and embracing. Stevens (1982) writes that she is

> Mother Nature and Earth Mother . . . the goddess of fertility and dispenser of nourishment; as water and sea she represents the origins of all life and is, as well, a symbol of the unconscious . . . as Moon Goddess she exemplifies the essential periodicity of womanhood. She also takes the form of divine animals: the bear (jealous guardian of her children), or the celestial cow who nourishes the earth with milky rain. [p. 89]

In Sandplay she is also depicted as mountains and/or caves, as well as certain types of animals (cows, bears, whales, pigs, etc.).

As the *Terrible Mother*, in her negative aspect, she can devour, destroy, and swallow everything up. She is the blood-stained goddess of death and destruction. She is sometimes seen in the form of Medusa, who turns men to stone. In Sandplay, she is often the Dragon that needs to be overcome, or an erupting volcano.

Another aspect of this archetype is that, when activated, it can become a way of controlling every relationship. The Great

Mother is also the mistress of guilt and her negative controlling side can become so extreme that it totally denies the essence of the other person.

Sandplay is particularly suited to problems with the Great Mother because of the use of the earth element of sand, which has the potential to link us directly to the realm of the Earth Mother in a tactile way. Healing then becomes possible by mediating in that earthy realm.

The *Wise Old Man,* often called the Senex, is the next archetype to consider. In his positive form, he has the wisdom of Solomon, a guru, or a savior. The recent advent of the Men's Movement draws heavily on this archetype. He can also be the *Puer Aeternis* in his negative aspect, the eternally youthful man who refuses to grow up but who lives his life in a devil-may-care fashion. These are often the patients we see who are beset with alcohol and/or drug problems and who live in denial. The puer is most often brought to therapy by another person because of continuing relationship difficulties. An additional negative aspect of the Wise Old Man is the *Inner Judge,* who is critical, demanding, noncomplimentary, and so on. He attacks the self-esteem of whomever he comes into contact with and is a terribly destructive force for many people.

The *Hero* is another major archetype, one that is frequently encountered in life and in Sandplay. The hero's main task is "to overcome the monster of darkness, to achieve victory over the powers of darkness, to bring the triumph of good over evil and the dominance of consciousness over the unconscious" (Wilmer 1991, p. 111).

Rites of passage and of initiation are associated with the mythological progression of the hero archetype. *Saint George and the Dragon,* a Christian myth, is often used as the model of the hero archetype. According to legend, St. George happened upon a town that was being terrorized by a dragon. The townspeople had offered the beast all of the town's sheep in an attempt to assuage its hunger. Eventually, when all the sheep were gone, they had to offer their own children. Finally, the lot fell to the king's daughter, who had been sent out to meet the dragon just prior to George's arrival. George rode out and confronted this beast, transfixed it with his lance, and saved the life of the princess.

The negative side of the hero is the *Trickster*, as seen in the myths of Hermes and Ulysses. The characteristics of the Trickster are chaotic caprice, malicious prankishness, and meddlesome, cunning wit. The Trickster is a nonconforming archetype; yet he also holds the shadow of the divine and demonic, good and evil.

The *Anima* is the feminine or contrasexual archetype in masculine psychology. It is the male's projection of his feminine ideal. When a man dreams of a woman who is not personally known to him, the figure can represent either positive or negative aspects of the dreamer's Anima. This can be either a helpful figure or a threatening one, but both are looked at as Anima projections. The positive Anima in men can often be seen as a beautiful, young, goddess-type woman, like Marilyn Monroe, or in her negative form as a nagging, bitchy shrew or witch, the supreme castrator.

The *Animus* is the term Jung used for women's projections of their contrasexual or masculine side. The Animus is seen as either supercontrolling, an Inner Judge, or a helpful male figure of some sort. For example, if a woman has a dream that her car breaks down on a dark and lonely road and a band of robbers sets upon her, that is an example of an overpowering, punishing, negative Animus state. If, on the other hand, a handsome man comes by and offers to fix the car for her, that would be considered the helpful or positive Animus.

The *Inner Child* archetype is the one most often repressed in the adult, yet is the part that holds the most promise for creative growth. The child archetype is a universal symbol of the unknowable but latent possibilities of the psyche. Most important, however, it symbolizes the present moment: the wonder, receptivity, and freshness of consciousness that is open to the here and now. The child embodies and encourages spontaneity and joy, imagination and celebration. Jung (1959) believed that the archetype of the child held the potential for all forms of creative thought. The Inner Child, then, can be seen as the divine child or, in its negative aspect, as an impish devil. Both are aspects of the child archetype and both are often seen in dreams and in Sandplay.

The *Ego/Self* archetype needs special consideration as, according to Jung, it is the central archetype in the collective unconscious. The Ego is ultimately located in the conscious realm of the psyche, while the Self is always buried deep within the unconscious. The Self, in Jungian terms, does not refer to the individual person, but rather, to the transpersonal, spiritual part of the personality with which a person is born. *The Child* (1973), by Neumann, discusses this aspect in great detail and demonstrates that the Ego and the Self of the child are contained within the deep recesses of the mother's psyche and only gradually does the child move into its own relationship to the Self. Jung (1959) considers the Self to be the central archetype of wholeness and totality. The numinous power inherent in the Ego/Self archetype comes from its ability to reconnect and center and, in this way, to balance opposites.

This reconnection sets the stage for the possibility of deep healing to occur. One of the basic postulates of Jungian psychology is that the psyche has the potential to heal itself, just as the body does, provided a space is made for this to occur. Dora Kalff and her students believe that through Sandplay this possibility can be activated. The sand tray, with its specified size and with the use of the earth element of sand, provides a symbolic vehicle for this to occur.

The Self appears in dreams, myths, fairy tales, and Sandplay. It is sometimes seen as the king, the queen, the hero, the prophet, the savior. It can also appear as the magic circle, the square, and the cross; it is the total union of the opposites, such as masculine and feminine, upper and lower, dark and light, past and future, and so on. The Self, when activated through Sandplay, is always felt as a balanced, serene moment and is experienced by the maker and the therapist as an "aha" moment. When the Ego/Self axis is constellated in Sandplay, it is truly a numinous experience. It is both visual and intensely felt.

The task of therapy is to set the stage that will allow the psyche to fulfill its mission, which is the unification of the conscious and unconscious aspects of the various archetypes as they are presented over time.

"The constellation of the self" (Kalff's phrase) can certainly be observed in Sandplay therapy and, when seen, is the signal to the therapist that true, deep healing is now possible. When that occurs, a union of the various masculine and feminine elements is illustrated. Present as well is a symbol of the Self, which often has a strong spiritual component. At times, this is an indescribable experience and, as discussed by Weinrib (1983), one that can only be felt. A note of caution, however: merely witnessing this phenomenon does not ensure that deep healing will occur, but it does set the possibility in motion. That is not the conclusion of the process of Sandplay Therapy, but it is a very positive signal that the Ego/Self archetype is ready for the final stage of integration. The Ego is now considered ready to mediate with the Self in a healthy way. It is never advisable to offer interpretations until one has witnessed concrete evidence of this phenomenon when doing Sandplay. This is the message to the therapist: the ego is now strong enough to accept interpretations. The work now shifts and becomes what Kalff called "the unfolding of the Self." It is now possible to mediate with the archetypes in a most constructive fashion.

Jung's theories of Psychological Types (1976) are also beneficial to an understanding of what is observed in Sandplay. Jung classified two overall personality dimensions, those of Introversion and Extraversion. Each of these dimensions has four personality preferences: thinking, feeling, sensation, and intuition. I believe that when one is able to study a sand scene from her own internal functions, the understanding of a scene is enhanced. For example, one consciously attends to what one *thinks* about a scene: "What do I *think* the maker is trying to convey to me?" Then, one can make a mental shift and ask, "What *sensation*-related message is in the scene? Are miniature selections, numbers, colors, the shape of the sand, the overall use of space important to an understanding of this picture?" Next, one can consider the *feeling* tone of the production: "What kind of *feeling* reaction do I get when I look at this scene? Is it happy? Is it upsetting? Is it confusing?" Last, one can shift to one's *intuitive* function and ask, "Do I get any *hints* of what might be needed next?" The attempt by the therapist to consciously attend to these elements can serve to enhance and deepen the work immeasurably. The analysis of the material is not shared with the maker. It is used solely for the therapist's analysis and understanding of the scene, which may be transmitted nonverbally to the client.

DORA KALFF

Lowenfeld's World Technique was incorporated into Jungian work through the efforts of Dora Kalff. During her training period at the Jung Institute in the early '50s, Kalff attended one of Dr. Lowenfeld's lectures. She was quite intrigued by the World Technique and discussed it with Dr. Jung. Jung remembered the positive impression that this technique had made upon him some years before, so he encouraged Frau Kalff to go to London to study with Dr. Lowenfeld, which she did in 1952.

From the beginning, Jung was a strong supporter of Kalff's work with children, as he had had the opportunity to observe her abilities first-hand. Kalff's children and Jung's grandchildren used to play together and he had noticed how happy his grandchildren seemed to be after they had visited the Kalff family. He had, in fact, commented to others about this. When Kalff began her analytic training, Jung encouraged her to work with children. Kalff's personal analysis during her training was with Emma Jung, Jung's wife.

After Kalff's studies with Lowenfeld in England, she returned to Switzerland and began to practice the Lowenfeld method while integrating it within her Jungian orientation. This was the first attempt at such a combination. She began to observe that there were certain developmental stages that were visible to her in the sand and she saw that the children she treated seemed to make rapid adjustments to whatever their presenting problems were. She felt that it was "almost as if an autonomous process was occurring with little or no interpretation being given by her" (Weinrib 1983, p. 15).

Kalff began her work with the Jungian postulate that there is a drive towards wholeness and healing in the human psyche, just as there is in the body. She saw the need for a free space in which this could happen, and she always referred to the sand tray as the "free and protected space," the *temenos* or place of healing. Kalff made no judgments about what she observed and used primarily a nonverbal approach, being careful to say nothing that might interfere with the child's process of psychological development. For this quiet, accepting attitude, she drew on her study of Zen Buddhism, which holds that a seeker is never to be given a direct answer to his most searching question. Instead, each person is encouraged to turn back to his own inner resource in order to discover his own authentic answer to whatever question is being explored.

Kalff believed that the unspoken understanding, the feeling connection, in other words the transference and countertransference dynamics, that develops between the analyst and the child is the ultimate healing factor (Kalff 1966). There is some controversy among Sandplay therapists about this issue, as there are those who hold that the transference is not to the person of the therapist but to the tray. In fact, Lowenfeld went to great lengths to discourage this phenomenon and was known to switch a child's therapist from time to time in order to ensure that the transference would be to the equipment rather than to the therapist. I, personally, find this idea appalling and am unsure whether this is the practice today.

ERICH NEUMANN

In Kalff's search to legitimize her work in a solid theoretical base, she had the opportunity to attend a lecture given by the German Jungian analyst Erich Neumann. In that lecture, he presented his theories of a child's psychological development. (These were published posthumously, in 1963, as *The Child*. The first English version of the book appeared in 1973.) Kalff recognized that Neumann's theories and her observations of the sand pictures of her young patients seemed to parallel and substantiate each other. The two met and discussed the possibility of doing joint research. Neumann's untimely death in 1960, however, precluded this collaboration.

A major focus of Neumann's research was the matriarchal level of consciousness (1954, 1955). As noted earlier, the medium of sand is directly linked to that early matriarchal level and, since sand is an earth element, it is particularly well suited as the medium for a symbolic grounding in the process of confronting problems arising from the Great Mother archetype.

Neumann recognized early on the importance of play in ego development. He writes in *The Child* (1973), "The world of play is of extreme importance not only for children but also for the adults of all cultures. . . . Only an individual embedded in this symbolic reality of play can become a complete human being" (p. 70).

Neumann's theories of psychological development are roughly broken down into five stages that were almost identical to examples witnessed by Kalff in her therapeutic work with children. It must be stressed, however, that these stages do not necessarily occur in a linear order but, rather, may be interwoven throughout a child's therapy.

Neumann's stages are adapted and described below:

1. *Chaos*—This is revealed as a very early undifferentiated ego mass; many elements are included in random, un-related fashion. Neumann associates this stage with the very early mother–child experience. This is the stage where the infant cannot distinguish himself from his mother. In Sandplay, everything is mass confusion.

2. *Animal/Vegetative*—A beginning step towards psycho-logical integration is revealed when animals and vege-tation begin to appear. Neumann viewed this stage as the beginning of a growth period where the child will learn to separate from the mother. We might term this the *rapprochement stage*, the beginning of object con-stancy. It is important to note that the type of animal selected is significant. Different stages of development are illustrated by the use of a primitive or a domestic animal. A dinosaur illustrates a much deeper level of psychic aggression than a horse or a cow.

3. *Fighting*—Conflict is usually illustrated between forces representing good and evil. At times, conflict between male and female is also illustrated. Fighting may be portrayed with the use of male and female animals as well as persons. This is the stage of the oedipal struggle, with castration anxiety and resolution of a sexual iden-tity. The beginning of superego development often ap-pears in scenes as well. These pictures are among the easiest to understand because the conflict is so clearly presented.

4. *Ego/Self Axis*—This is the point when the ego and the Self are in a good relationship. This heralds the comple-

tion of a separate identity for the child. He knows now the I–Thou concept. He is a fully separate human being from his mother. The ego is fully operative and the child has an inner Self concept. Prior to this stage, the Self of the child has been contained within the mother. Now he has integrated and balanced the union of the opposites (often masculine and feminine). This development signals that the ego and the Self are now related in a meaningful way. In Sandplay, this stage is illustrated by a sense of balance and serenity, and often the masculine and feminine opposites are depicted. In most cases the scene has a spiritual dimension, and the pictures are viewed by both the maker and the therapist with a sense of awe.

5. *Adaptation to the Collective*—This is a scene reflective of normal everyday life. Neumann considered this the stage when the child is ready to start a relationship with the world: going to school, experiencing peer relationships, anything that heralds a worldview beyond the early maternal relationship. When seen in Sandplay, this stage signals to the therapist that the child is ready to resume his life in the world and that termination is not far off.

Kalff called the fourth step, the ego/Self connection, the *constellation of the Self*. She regarded this as a critical point in therapy, for it demonstrated and illustrated to her that the ego and the Self were now reunited in a readily visible medium. This is considered a critical developmental stage because of the theory that the ego/Self axis of everyone has been separated and wounded in early life (by virtue of the birth trauma) and thus is the basis for neurotic afflictions. Once the ego and the Self are again in good relationship, the possibility exists for a deeper healing to occur. Kalff also used this concept as a signal that now the ego would be able to accept therapeutic interpretations. Prior to witnessing this phenomenon in a patient, she would serve primarily as a silent observer of the process. This does not mean that she did not interact with the child, but that her interpretations were not offered.

OTHER IMPORTANT CONTRIBUTIONS

Eric Homberger Erikson had never met or heard of Lowenfeld (Mitchell and Friedman 1994), but his experiments were done around the same time that she was formulating her theories. Erikson had been a poor student and barely finished high school. He never went to college. This is quite remarkable, given his many contributions to the field. During his search for his life's work, he took a teaching assignment in Vienna at a clinic run by Anna Freud and was fortunate to undergo a training analysis with her in the 1930s. He became a psychoanalyst and was later appointed professor at Harvard, where he developed the Dramatic Productions Test (Homberger 1938). This test asked college students to use a collection of miniatures to create a scene and then to make up a moving picture story for it. The scene was constructed on a table top, but did not use sand. In almost every case, the instructions were ignored by the students. Instead, what emerged were scenes in symbolic form that could be connected to traumatic events from the subjects' own childhoods. Erikson's interpretation was that these students, when confronted with toys, regressed to the age in childhood when the trauma had occurred and attempted to overcome these traumatic experiences through an active repetition in play. In other words, they immediately regressed to the level of the trauma in order to rework it. Erikson's later studies pinpointed differences in masculine and feminine psychology through his observations of the toys chosen to depict scenes of males and females.

Edward Edinger (1972) diagrammed how the ego evolves from the Self, which is located in the collective unconscious (see Diagram 1–1). In his description of this process, Edinger speaks of the Self as the ordering and unifying principle of the psyche, while the ego is the center of the conscious personality. The Self is the inner empirical deity or the spiritual center. He affirms that the ego is embedded in the Self and

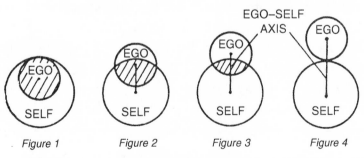

| Figure 1 | Figure 2 | Figure 3 | Figure 4 |

Diagram 1–1.

gradually, throughout life, it achieves full separation. Edinger goes on to say that this is a lifelong process, and the diagram refers to the entire life of an individual. He describes the stages as follows:

> Figure 1 corresponds to Neumann's original uroboric state. . . . Ego and Self are one, which means that there is no ego. This is the total state of primary ego–Self identity. (The uroborus is an ancient symbol of a serpent bent in a circle and biting its own tail. It represents the primordial Self out of which ego consciousness is born [Stevens 1982].)
>
> Figure 2 shows an emerging ego which is beginning to separate but which still has its center and greater area in primary identity with the Self.
>
> Figure 3 presents a more advanced stage of development. . . . The ego–Self axis, which . . . has now become partly conscious.
>
> Figure 4 is an ideal theoretical limit which probably does not exist in actuality. It represents a total separation of ego and Self and a complete consciousness of the ego–Self axis. [p. 6]

Edinger goes on to postulate that because of the early wounding to the psyche, the ego–Self axis is broken, and the task of therapy is to reunite the ego and the Self in some meaningful way. It is his belief that everyone experiences wounding as a result of the early separation of mother and child, and that the personality can only achieve wholeness by repairing this early trauma.

Edinger's diagram is an overall lifeview, illustrating a cyclical process that continues over time. When one puts it into a childhood schema, it is directly related to child personality development, particularly for the first few years of life.

PRESENT STATE OF SANDPLAY THERAPY

Until the last ten or fifteen years, it had been quite difficult for therapists in this country to obtain Sandplay training and supervision. During Kalff's lifetime, she provided some training in California, under the aegis and support of the San Francisco Jung Institute. This organization was instrumental in introducing Kalff to this country and in bringing her here periodically. As a result, many Sandplay practitioners were trained by Kalff on the West Coast, and that is why so many Sandplay practitioners are located there. I attended several of Kalff's workshops in California. The other way to obtain training was to travel to Switzerland and study with Kalff there, which some of us did.

Today there are various training opportunities for interested therapists to pursue. One source is the International Society of Sandplay Therapists (ISST). This was founded by Kalff shortly before her death, along with several influential Sandplay therapists in the United States and Europe. Among them were Estelle Weinrib in New York and Kay Bradway in California. They spearheaded the branch known as Sandplay Therapists of America (STA). The requirement for an American membership in ISST is accreditation through STA.

In Europe, Martin Kalff leads the European branch of ISST and has continued the work that his mother began. Frau Kalff also trained many Japanese therapists and today there is a large contingent of Sandplay therapists in Japan and Hawaii. The focus of these organizations is on ensuring that interested practitioners are trained in a strict "Kalffian" approach. The guidelines for training and supervision are quite strict, with the result that the membership is rather small when one considers the large number of therapists who are presently using this medium.

Other sources are available to meet the needs of therapists who want training but are not interested in the strict Jungian/ Kalffian approach. Gisela DeDomenico, in California, offers training for therapists who have different levels of experience. Her background is both Jungian and Lowenfeldian. On the East Coast, I run training groups and offer supervision through a Jungian theoretical base. Both DeDomenico and I offer on-site training in other parts of the country and we are both accredited play therapy supervisors of the Association for Play Therapy (APT). The APT, through its annual international conferences, has added significantly to the popularity of and exposure to Sandplay methodology. Since Sandplay with children is essentially a play therapy technique, each of the APT conferences offers a number of presentations on Sandplay for different levels of experience and different orientations.

It is essential that anyone interested in Sandplay become aware of the resources that exist and avail themselves of training and supervision in this modality. It is also essential that one experience Sandplay personally before using it with clients. Sandplay is a very powerful medium that requires a thorough grounding in theory, as well as adequate personal exposure, if it is to be practiced effectively.

Jungians are firm believers in the tenet that you can only take a client as far as you have been able to go yourself. This holds true in Sandplay, in dream analysis, in art therapy, or in any other form of therapy. Experience is the best teacher.

Sandplay is not suitable for all therapists. It is meant for those who feel inexorably drawn to its power and who are willing to take the time and effort to pursue it responsibly. It is a demanding tool to use, in every sense of the word, and takes much drive and dedication, but it also holds the promise of a deep inner connectedness to one's basic psychological core. This is true for therapist and client alike, which is why therapists need to experience Sandplay personally before using it with clients. It offers a medium that can unite the ego and the Self in a visible, creative, enduring, and life-enhancing way.

✥ 2 ✥

Introduction to Sandplay Therapy with Families

Sandplay with families draws on several theoretical bases: play therapy, family therapy, and Sandplay therapy. The major difference between Sandplay with individuals and with families is in the theory, interventions, and interpretations that are used. This chapter will discuss the histories and theories of play therapy and family therapy in order to show how family sandplay therapy has developed and how it can effectively incorporate the tenets of those earlier modalities.

PLAY THERAPY

While Sigmund Freud is credited with the first case of child therapy, play therapy itself has a history that dates back to the 1920s. Most of the cases treated in the twenties and thirties were either in a psychoanalytic setting or in child guidance centers.

The Association for Play Therapy, spearheaded by Charles Schaefer and Kevin O'Connor in 1982, has grown from a modest beginning to a membership that now numbers over 3000. This organization established a registration process for play therapists and play therapy supervisors that ensures that adequate standards are met before one can use the title Play Therapist or Play Therapy Supervisor. Similar accrediting organizations have been established in Canada and other parts of the world.

Historically, play therapy has not been recognized as a distinct treatment modality for children, but has been and continues to be subsumed under the rubric of psychotherapy or psychoanalysis. For example, a clinician who treats individual children cannot submit "play therapy" to an insurance company when describing what is being provided. The modality of family therapy has finally been accepted by third-party payors so perhaps, in the future, play therapy will eventually also be accepted. The therapist who treats children alone must still use "psychotherapy" for the definition.

Today more and more clinicians are using play therapy techniques to work with young patients and their families. However, each case calls for a thorough diagnosis and assessment of both the individual child and the child in the context of his family system. No single approach to treatment is suitable for every situation. In some instances, such as those seen in some child guidance centers, parents are included in parent counseling sessions while the children receive individual or group therapy. This often occurs in those cases where it becomes clear that the parents need parenting skills before any other type of therapy with them can be utilized.

Some of the better known methods of play therapy in use today are described below. I am not espousing any of these methods over others, but have chosen to illustrate several which may be of interest to the reader.

Filial Therapy, developed by Louise and Bernard Guerney (1964, 1966), teaches specific therapeutic techniques for parents to use at home with their children. The parents are offered this modality only after a careful assessment of the child and the family to determine its appropriateness. Through a series of group training sessions, the parents are taught treatment techniques and are provided with ongoing parental group support. This method is especially useful because it puts the parents in charge of their child's therapy and it is generally well received. Using this approach, most parents feel they are not only the cause of the problem but are also directly involved in the solution. This results in much more positive parent–child interaction. Another benefit is that it allows parents to become more effective in their parenting, which enhances their self-esteem. Far too often, parents feel they are failures if their child needs therapy. This is addressed and minimized in Filial Therapy.

Behaviorism sprang from the work of B. F. Skinner, and uses a token reward system for behavioral problems. This technique is often taught to parents needing help with specific problems, such as bedwetting. For each night that bedwetting does not occur, the child attaches a star to a chart that was made by the parent and child together. A reward is earned by the accumulation of a specified number of stars. It is usually helpful to make the early rewards somewhat easier to attain than later ones. For example, the attainment of five stars might be the goal at the beginning of treatment, with a gradual addition to the number of stars required before the next reward is provided. The child and the parent decide together what the reward will be. The prize need not be a concrete item, but should be geared to the child's age and interests. For example, the reward might be that the child is allowed to stay up an hour later than usual one night, or to watch a movie. Later on, it might be a special outing with the parents, with no siblings included. It is suggested that there be no monetary reward. The major reward is the child's intrinsic feeling of mastery, which is a significant accomplishment in itself. There is no penalty on those occasions when the child is not successful. This method is often adapted for use in schools for behavioral problems. It rewards only positive behaviors and ignores negative behaviors, with the goal being to encourage positive behaviors and to extinguish negative ones. Behaviorism has been well utilized in cases of serious developmental delays, but is certainly beneficial in less difficult situations as well.

Theraplay is a relatively recent technique developed by Ann Jernberg (1989), who adapted this approach from the work of Austin Des Lauriers (1962) and Viola Brody (1993). The technique is quite directive, and in this approach the therapist essentially employs regression. She takes the child back to the earliest developmental stages in order to assist the child with a positive resolution of that period. She then moves to each successive developmental stage, until all the blocks to mastery have been conquered. In this approach, touch is the primary healing agent. All humans are born with the innate need to make contact with the other through touch. The baby's first experience of the mother is that of being held and nurtured by her. In Theraplay, the therapist *becomes* the mother and uses maternal body contact methods such as kissing toes, tickling, hugging, rocking, and singing to the child. There are times when the need arises to use punitive methods, such as firmly restraining the child from hurting himself or the therapist. Strong stress is laid on the fact that touch is normal, and through touch a child learns what is pleasurable as well as what is unacceptable. This method is designed to mimic all forms of early parent–child interactions. The Theraplay therapist maintains control of the situation at all times through this directive method. The only problem with this technique is the conflict today over touching or not touching a patient, one that each therapist must struggle with if she chooses to use this technique.

Child-Centered Play Therapy is yet another approach. The distinguishing focus is the attitude that the therapist brings to the play therapy experience. It is an attitude that we hope is a basic personality trait of most therapists and one that honors fully the person of the child in all her vagaries. Garry Landreth (1991) wrote about the qualities needed by a therapist: "Genuineness or realness implies that the therapist possesses a high degree of self-understanding and self-acceptance and is congruent in what is being felt and what is being expressed in the relationship" (p. 65). A therapist possessing these qualities is able to value the child for herself and for whatever she brings to the situation. The child is not criticized or reprimanded or made to feel guilt or fear, but is made to feel fully and completely accepted. This allows her to eventually internalize her own sense of self-acceptance and self-worth. Child-centered play therapy has its roots in the philosophies of Rogers and Axline but is also directly linked with the Jungian tenet that the psyche has its own built-in striving towards wholeness.

Garry Landreth (1991), as cited above, and Clark Moustakas (1953, 1975, 1981) have been major proponents of the child-centered focus. Landreth says that "Child-centered play therapy is an attitude, a philosophy, and a way of being" (p. 55). He goes on to say, "This kind of acceptance and warm caring is characterized by a positive respect for the child as a person of worth" (p. 66). An attitude of acceptance and respect is always present and is of inestimable value when the time comes to include the parents and the rest of the family in the therapeutic process. When one includes other family members, the process might be termed *child-centered family treatment*. One example is those cases where child treatment alone cannot ameliorate the stress that a child is experiencing within the family. If the child is included in the family therapy, it should only be after she has made sufficient progress to tolerate the kind of anxiety that is to be anticipated when she must confront the parents and other family members, and when she feels fully supported by the therapist.

There are other equally well-respected therapeutic approaches that treat children, such as Object Relations, Gestalt, and psychoanalytic. Each theory has its own adherents and each its own successes. It is important that every therapist adhere primarily to her own philosophy and recognize that no single theory can be applied to all cases. Most therapists use several theories, dependent on the presenting problem. This carries over to the use of sandplay, as well. I am primarily a Jungian, but I also use family systems when families are included.

The role of the parents needs special consideration in all approaches, since children do not live in a vacuum and do, in almost all cases, return to their homes at the end of each therapeutic hour. This reality has presented therapists with challenges since the very beginning of child therapy. Success or failure can often be contingent upon the therapist's relationship to the parents as well as to the child. I include parents on a monthly basis, to keep contact with them and to obtain their invaluable feedback on the child's progress at home. If and when the appropriate time comes to shift to a family therapy format, the parents have already experienced a positive relationship with me.

PIONEERS OF PLAY THERAPY

Sandplay with children is a technique that incorporates theories of play therapy. Therefore, a brief survey of some of the early pioneers of play therapy and some of their contributions follows.

Virginia Axline (1947) worked closely with Carl Rogers and adopted his techniques in her child cases. She used a reflective process, commenting on what she was observing or reflecting back to the child what the child was doing, for example, "I see you've chosen the mother doll," or, when anger has been expressed, "That really makes you feel angry." Axline was psychoanalytically oriented and believed that the child had the inherent ability to handle his own problems without parents always being included. She wrote, *"It is not necessary for the adults to be helped in order to insure successful play therapy results"* (1947, p. 66, Axline's italics).

Melanie Klein (1959), another early pioneer, was also psychoanalytically based. She used an analysis of the transference as the basic core of her work and believed that interpretation was essential in treatment. She saw play as a free-association process and thus open to interpretation. Klein initially held sessions in the child's home, but after some experiments felt this had a detrimental effect because the child could not feel free to express himself in this setting. This led to Klein's belief that parents were intrusive in the transference relationship, so she eliminated contact with them entirely.

Anna Freud (1946) was another psychoanalytically based theorist whose approach differed from Klein's in that she avoided direct interpretations. She preferred that the child come to his own observations when he was ready to do so. Like Klein, she believed that the transference was important, but it was not the central focus of the analysis. Freud believed that it was important to maintain contact with the parents.

Margaret Lowenfeld was a prominent child therapist, as well as the forerunner of Sandplay. Her contributions were discussed in Chapter One.

Klein, Freud, and Lowenfeld practiced in London in the twenties and thirties, while Axline practiced in the United States. Each one made significant yet different contributions to the field of play therapy. There are many others who have had a strong impact on child therapy, such as D. W. Winnicott and Michael Fordham. The list could go on and on.

My orientation is a meld of many of those mentioned above. I use a child-centered, noninterpretive, nondirective approach and include either parent counseling or family play therapy, as dictated by the requirements of each case.

FAMILY THERAPY MODELS AND PIONEERS

Until quite recently, family therapists excluded children under the age of 10 or 12 from family therapy, based on the assumption that they were too young to understand or that they might be exposed to parental issues that had nothing to do with them. A special edition of the *Family Therapy Networker* (Author unknown 1991) recognized this as a serious omission and encouraged family therapists to rethink their position on the matter and look for ways to include the younger family members. Aside from the expressed reservations about a child's ability to tolerate family therapy, there may have been other reasons children were excluded, such as the therapist's lack of training in how to work with children or the therapist's fear that the child would make a mess in her office. For some therapists, having small children present brought up unresolved conflicts from their own childhoods.

Ibrahim Orgun (1973), for example, recommended holding therapy sessions in a playroom rather than an office setting, noting that children under 10 feel more comfortable in the playroom and that adults more readily communicate their willingness to listen to children in that setting than in a more formal office. He also asserts that meeting in an office raises the anxiety level of a child (and often of adults as well); when the session is held in the playroom, anxiety can be discharged through the play materials. Another advantage of using the playroom is that it helps the parents understand what play therapy is all about.

I believe it may be more comfortable for the play therapist to include families than it is for the family therapist to include young children because the play therapist is more attuned to the disruptive aspects that occur in a playroom setting than is a traditional family therapist.

Following are some observations about the history of family therapy which have been adapted from two books, one by

William Nichols and Craig Everett (1986), the other by Fred P. Piercy, Douglas H. Sprenkle, Joseph L. Wetchler, and associates (1996).

According to Nichols and Everett (1986), family therapy sprang up in various places at about the same time, so that no single person or movement can take credit. Because it arose from multiple sources, it developed into a very complex picture. Much of the early family work was focused on the schizophrenic patient and the interplay between the patient and his family. Today, with recent research, schizophrenia is viewed as a metabolic disorder and is treated by medication, family support, and education. As a result, it appears that a large number of schizophrenic patients are treated by psychiatrists in order that hospitalization and/or medication can be prescribed and monitored. There continues to be ongoing debate about this, however, with some practitioners insisting that the cause is environmental rather than metabolic.

Family therapy was practiced as far back as the 1920s and 1930s. The first clinics to focus on marital and family counseling were established around 1930. In 1932, Columbia University opened the Family Consultation Service of Child Development, through Teachers College. Other agencies in cities such as Boston, Philadelphia, and Cleveland were also developing services for children and families.

As the family therapy field progressed, new views constantly came into play. One important area of work that has appeared within the past ten to fifteen years is based on a feminist perspective of the family.

A study conducted by Gurman and colleagues (1985) found that "approximately 71 percent of the cases of childhood and/ or adolescent behavioral problems treated by any one of several well-defined family therapy approaches or by eclectic methods can be expected to improve" (Nichols and Everett 1986, pp. 59–60). This suggests to me that therapists should use the theoretical framework within which they, personally, are most comfortable.

With the development of family therapy, different theorists became associated with different schools of thought. The major divisions were known as the *structural*, the *strategic*, the *psychodynamic*, the *communicationist*, and the *systemic*. However, there was a great deal of overlap among all these various schools. By combining different aspects from two or three schools, practitioners attempted to correct the problem of being strictly associated with one view or the other, and began to refer to themselves as *interactive* or *integrative*. A brief review of some of these models follows.

Psychodynamic

Therapists using this model are more oriented to individual therapy, but occasionally see families. Lyman Wynne, an early psychodynamic practitioner, observed that the carefully constructed and maintained facade of a happy family often covers a situation of very serious conflicts, a situation he referred to as *pseudomutuality*. He found that outsiders were kept from penetrating the system, making therapy with this type of family quite difficult.

Nathan Ackerman, often referred to as the "founding father of family therapy" (Nichols and Everett 1986, p. 43), was a child psychiatrist in a child guidance clinic. Ackerman became dissatisfied with the psychoanalytic approach because he felt that it omitted whole segments of the patient's life. He began to include family members as part of the overall child treatment. Ackerman was known to stress the importance of the therapist's personality as one of the primary determinants of success or failure in therapy. He felt that the special fit of a given family with a given therapist was more important than any theoretical orientation held by the therapist. This view is also held by Landreth and many others in the child therapy field.

Strategic

Fred Piercy and Joseph Wetchler (1996) record the development of strategic family therapy and structural family therapy by noting that they were born on different coasts of the United States around the same time.

> Strategic family therapy has its roots in the Palo Alto research group led by Gregory Bateson in the early 1950s. . . . Bateson began to focus on schizophrenia . . . [and to] influence therapists throughout the country to examine the double-binding communications of family members. . . . Strategic family therapy is characterized by the use of specific strategies for addressing family problems . . . through straightforward or paradoxical directives. [pp. 50–51]

Nichols and Everett (1986) comment, "Strategic family therapy focuses on communication in the present and uses directives from the therapist to change behavior" (p. 56).

Jay Haley and Chloe Madanes were two of the major proponents of the strategic model. Haley's work in the 1950s and Madanes's in the 1980s were early examples of brief family therapy, as was that of Don Jackson, Paul Watzlawick, and John Weakland. They were all directive and behavioral in their approach and drew heavily on communication theory.

Structural

The structural school of family therapy began in a residential institution for ghetto boys in New York. Salvador Minuchin and his colleagues worked at the Wiltwyck School for boys and served their families as well, a population that came primarily from New York's inner-city ghettos. When discussing the structural school, Piercy and Wetchler (1996) describe how the issues for these boys and their families were ones of immediacy and survival and were not amenable to a long-term, psychoanalytic approach. Minuchin discovered that using a structural approach to family therapy, rather than a psychoanalytic model, was much more effective with this population. "This is done with a focus on the present, using direct, indirect, and paradoxical directives" (p. 53). The structural method, then, focuses on patterns of interaction in the present and is also derived from communication theory. The strategic and structural are more alike than different.

The structuralists pay particular attention to the hierarchy that exists in families, and attempt to restructure the family system. This is often attempted through paradoxical means. For example, in argumentative situations a family is told to go home and keep arguing, but to argue more loudly and more often than they were presently doing. The structuralists believe that families recognize how ridiculous this "prescription" is and refuse to do the assignment altogether.

Communicationist

I believe that this theory is related to and incorporated into all the other schools. The communicationists consider such things as who talks the most, who talks the least, who is the loudest, and who distracts to be of paramount importance. Equal attention is paid to the verbal and the nonverbal aspects of communication. Special attention is paid to self-selected seating arrangements, body movements, facial expressions, and overall affect. Communication theorists such as Don Jackson, Jay Haley, and Virginia Satir assert that family communication patterns are designed as a system of power and control.

Virginia Satir (1964), who was often called the mother of family therapy, believed that the inclusion of all members of a family in therapy meant that preventive work was being done with the siblings of the identified patient. This is seen in many cases where, during therapy, one family member improves but symptoms often crop up in another. Satir began by scheduling two sessions with the marital pair, in order to strengthen them as individuals and as mates, before she moved to include the children.

Some other pioneer theorists of the communicationist approach were Milton Erickson, Carlos Montalvo, and John Weakland. Each has made significant contributions to the field of family therapy. There have been many other contributors to the field of family therapy and the author apologizes for any omissions.

Systemic

The systemic therapists look at families as a system, an approach which was adapted from Ludwig von Bertalanffy's General Systems Theory (1962). Bertalanffy was a biologist whose ideas were published in 1945 and broadly accepted by the scientific community. The systemic theory says that relationships are governed by the system within which they operate. A system is something that is put together in such a way that whatever affects one part of it affects other parts as well. A useful analogy is to think of a fully blown-up balloon as being a well-functioning family. Imagine that pressure is applied to a specific part of the balloon. The result is that the balloon changes its shape to accommodate to the pressure. When the pressure becomes too strong, the balloon bursts and collapses. This is a way to visualize what one sees when a family is in crisis or when it is a dysfunctional one. The pressure is the stress or the presenting problem, and the stronger the pressure the more in danger the family is.

Murray Bowen's (1978) approach, a systemic one often referred to as "Bowenian," was to select the one person in the family who he felt was the healthiest and to do family therapy with that person. His rationale was that the healthiest member would have the most influence on changing the overall family system. It was Bowen who developed the theory of *triangles*. He viewed triangles as the building blocks of an emotional system that serves to bind individuals together. Triangles exist to maintain family homeostasis, thereby attempting to control family anxiety. When family triangles are identified by the therapist, that enables the family to address the underlying issues. This was, and continues to be, a major dynamic in family therapy as well as in family play therapy. One example of a triangled family that I treated was that of an intact family with a 12-year-old daughter and an 8-year-old son. The daughter had been identified much earlier as "the problem" and both parents believed if they could control her all the family problems would disappear. The daughter was in a special school and had received therapy from numerous practitioners. I was later asked to treat the son. I began with the boy initially, before moving to a family therapy format. The triangles that existed were numerous. Mom and Dad were allied against each child. Mom and the children were allied against Dad's punitive measures; yet when Mom was over-wrought, she called Dad home to administer his abusive methods of control. The work of therapy was to disentangle the various mixed messages that resulted in different forms of triangling. I felt one major accomplishment was the time Mom decided that she would have to handle conflicts between herself and the children alone, without calling Dad home, since she disapproved of his methods.

The field of family therapy, no matter which school one is allied with, is similar to and yet different from other types of therapy. There is the added need to understand the concepts and patterns that are discernible in families, such as the verbal and nonverbal messages being sent, the interactive process, the triangles that can be identified, or the apparent parentification or scapegoating of one member.

The *parentified child* (Nichols and Everett 1986) is one who takes over a parental role with a sibling or sometimes with a parent. He often develops symptoms such as adolescent depression, school phobia, separation problems, or emotional flatness. Any of these symptoms indicates underlying problems in the marital interaction.

The *scapegoated child* (Nichols and Everett 1986) is sometimes known as the "black sheep," the troublemaker, the one who deviates from the family norm. She carries the symptoms outside of the family system and engages in school misbehavior, sexual acting out, or delinquency. Unity in the family is achieved by scapegoating this one member.

Nichols and Everett (1986) illustrate that, in family therapy, attention also needs to be directed to the power that exists in the various subsystems (marital, parent–child, sibling). Boundary issues are also important in determining such things as whether this is a closed or open family system. A *closed* system is one in which the family binds together to keep others outside. There is an unspoken understanding in these families that strangers are not to be trusted. One often sees a closed system when a family is referred to a therapist by an outside agency, such as the court system. An *open* system, on the other hand, is one in which a basic level of trust has been established, enabling the family members to interact with outsiders. In the open type of family system, therapy is often initiated by the family itself.

BASIC PREMISES FOR FAMILY THERAPY

All family therapy is based on a few simple premises. First, of course, is that when a family comes for therapy someone feels that this family needs help. Sometimes the referral comes from a community agency, such as a school or the court system. It can be somewhat more difficult to break through the initial resistance in this type of case than if a family itself feels that it is in trouble and seeks help on its own. A family is always in a state of flux, always changing, always in a process of becoming. The family seen one week is not the same family that was seen the preceding week or that will be seen the following week.

Nichols and Everett (1986) cite eight basic questions to be addressed in family therapy:

1. What are the strengths in the family that need to continue or to change?

2. Where should separateness or connectedness be encouraged?
3. Is there enmeshment or disengagement?
4. Are communication patterns healthy or dysfunctional?
5. Is parentification in evidence?
6. Is scapegoating occurring?
7. Are there family myths and/or secrets?
8. Who holds the power in the family? [pp. 129–140]

With this background information on family therapy and play therapy, family play therapy is the logical next step.

Family Play Therapy

The following observations about family play therapy are drawn from a variety of sources, some of them cited by Wendy Miller (1994). There is a growing consensus in the field that using play in family therapy has a positive outcome. It decreases anxiety in the parents, as well as in the children, because it is so very natural to families. Every family engages in some sort of play activity at times.

Both family therapy and play therapy place heavy emphasis on the use of *metaphor*: children express themselves through the metaphor of play rather than verbally confronting their parents, which is much more intimidating. Their drawings, doll play, and such reveal to the therapist just what the problem is, and the family play therapist must be able to think and speak in metaphors to be fully effective. For example, when a child has chosen dolls to enact a drama in a doll house, the therapist must be careful to speak about the dolls in the language of the child. If the doll character is a mother, it is always referred to as the mother in the drama and not as the child's actual mother. By exploring the feelings of the child doll in the given situation, one can be sure there is a relationship to the actual child. This technique allows the child to express herself in a safer way rather than to talk about problems being experienced with the actual mother.

The therapist needs to understand child development, family stages, and individual, family, and group processes in order to be an effective healer. It is important for him to be able to join, to observe, to model, and to set limits when that becomes necessary. Most of all, the therapist must be sensitive, creative, spontaneous, directive when necessary, and always in charge of the process. This covers a large territory but these are skills and qualities that most therapists manage to acquire with experience. It is essential for the family play therapist to have training and experience with both family and play therapy techniques before attempting to combine the two. The major requirement, however, is a willingness to experiment with a new technique and to use oneself as creatively as possible. One needs to realize that perfection (whatever that might be) is not the goal, but that sincerity and openness to what each family is trying to resolve become the keys to success.

Some family therapists recognize that the omission of younger children in treatment has had deleterious results. The authors included in Schaefer and Carey's (1994) book are therapists who have attempted to correct this problem by using their own creative approaches, and each of these approaches has proved valid and effective.

My own theoretical preference when family play therapy is chosen is to focus on the family using a systems lens. I also rely heavily on communication theory, verbal as well as nonverbal, when attempting to assess a family. Pathology in this model is seen as the result of certain processes in the family system that cause stress on the individual, as described in the balloon analogy noted earlier. For example, if a father is out of work, stress is inevitable between the parents and often goes unexpressed. Mother does not feel that she can get angry at Dad because of the unemployment situation (provided it is not his fault). The child picks up Mom's anger unconsciously, begins to act out that anger in school, and is then referred for therapy. The child is not the problem in this case; the unemployment is. The child becomes the spokesperson for the family and is the agent that helps the family into treatment. This type of example is seen in other situations as well—certainly when alcohol, drug abuse, sexual abuse, or violence is the issue.

Other theoretical approaches to the field of family play therapy and the therapists who are associated with them are:

1. Object Relations (Scharff and Scharff 1987)
2. Integrative (Wachtel 1992)
3. Psychodynamic (Keith and Whitaker 1981)
4. Gestalt (Oaklander 1978)
5. Filial (Guerney et al. 1966)

My preferred modality is child-centered play therapy that also includes families at times. I have referred to this as *child-centered family play therapy*. The focus in this method is upon building a strong relationship with the child before moving into the family arena. In this approach, both play therapy and family play therapy are used.

I especially like Jill Scharff's (1989) discussion of the *holding capacity* and feel that it deserves mention. It is relevant to working with families in family play therapy and with children in child-centered play therapy. Every therapist symbolically "holds" families during the time that a family spends in therapy. This takes place from the initial moment of contact between the therapist and the family member who has made the first phone call until the final termination session. This contextual holding capacity must include the therapist's comfort with play, which includes noise, mess, regression, and sometimes surprises—all the features of normal family life. I vividly remember one session I had a couple of years ago. A family I was treating arrived with a 5-day-old infant in an infant carrier. Unknown to me, the baby had arrived early and they decided to surprise me by keeping their regularly scheduled appointment!

Many other family therapists believed that it was important to include the young child in family therapy. Ackerman (mentioned earlier) was one of the prime innovators in this area, along with David Keith and Carl Whitaker (1981). Joan Zilbach (1989) was also one of these proponents. Her contribution was to demonstrate that there are stages in the family life cycle that are as important to consider as the child's developmental stages and that all of this information should be included in the assessment process.

I do not believe, nor do I mean to imply, that every family should always be seen in a family play therapy format. There are reasons for excluding children at times, particularly when specific issues such as sexual problems emerge between the parents. This needs to be understood, especially with respect to the child's developmental level. One example that comes to mind is a situation where a parent has changed his or her sexual orientation when the child is just forming his or her own sexual identity. To explore this in a family format could be very damaging to the child. Another situation when a young child should be excluded is if a parent has threatened suicide or is in the midst of a psychotic episode. There are other circumstances when it is unwise to include the young child, but those judgments are therapeutic decisions.

I am strongly oriented towards a child-centered approach, which is not particularly compatible with the present thrust toward short-term therapy. Managed care, which focuses on a short-term contract, is a reality that all therapists face today. I am aware of this fact and am writing with that in mind. We can only do what is possible within the time allotted. However, when using a child-centered approach, after sufficient stabilization of the presenting problem has been achieved and a good level of trust has been established between the child and me, my work often moves to a family systems format that includes sandplay.

Some suggestions to keep in mind when assessing a family for family therapy are just as important to consider when one assesses a family for play therapy. Nichols and Everett (1986) suggest the following:

1. Make note of your clinical impressions of each family member's individual development with regard to maturity, personality integration, ego development, capacity for intimacy and bonding, and management of stress and anxiety.
2. Evaluate interpersonal dynamics within the spousal, parent/child, and sibling subsystems. This would include patterns of coalitions, triangles, parentification,

scapegoating, internal and external boundaries, and enmeshment/disengagement.
3. Identify broad family system and transgenerational patterns such as myths, secrets, and coalitions.
4. Characterize the system's social network patterns including residential environment, career, school, religious, and other social contacts. [p. 210]

Family Sandplay Therapy

Therapists often do not fully appreciate how much information is offered to them nonverbally. For example, when a child chooses to use a doll house, she arranges the furniture, then she rearranges it, and finally selects which characters are to live there. These actions are all nonverbal communications and can offer to the observant therapist insight into this particular child's thinking and feeling response to the material.

1. Are the rooms crammed full or empty of furniture?
2. Are only female or male figures chosen?
3. Are the rooms set up in a logical way?
4. What is the child's affect?

All of these things, and more, are important in order to understand a child's play.

When a family is being treated in sandplay, the members are frequently quite amazed by the nonverbal aspect of what has been produced in their sand pictures. Their observations at the conclusion of the session often refer to their sense of astonishment. Especially revealing are the decision-making process, the alliances that are established, the choices that are made, and the family interactions. When the family has completed the picture, there may be much oohing and aahing over what has been produced and the family members may discuss their visceral reactions. The internally felt power that results from the construction of a sand picture is quite moving to the family and the therapist alike.

The preceding pages have offered background information on sandplay, play therapy, and family therapy. When all of these techniques are combined, the result is family sandplay therapy. There has been very little written about this modality. I have written one of the few articles to date (Carey 1991). Some of the points made in this article are the following:

Sandplay and family therapy, when combined, offer a variety of possibilities for further study.

1. Because of the dimensions of the sandbox, limits are both physically and symbolically set. This can provide a containment for families where boundaries are a problem. Members can learn to particularize their own dilemma while, at the same time, they learn a new way to accomplish integration and communication.
2. Family alliances can be observed by the therapist through the choices made, such as who chooses to work with whom, which miniatures are selected and by whom, and so forth. These choices can offer an opportunity to intervene by restructuring destructive alliances into healthier ones, and can thus provide a more objective view to the family, by interventions offered by the therapist.

3. Unconscious contents are rapidly revealed to the therapist as well as to the family and make it possible to discuss some of the patterns as they emerge. In this way, more conscious choices are suggested and can be implemented within the therapy.
4. Sandplay appeals to the children in a family and offers reparative work to the "inner child" of each parent as well.
5. The uniqueness of each family can be observed in the spiritual strivings that are revealed, in the sense of the family as a life force as these are seen in each individual as well as in the family unit. [pp. 237–238]

In addition to what has been discussed previously, family sandplay therapy also borrows from the ideas of art therapy, particularly those of Helen Landgarten. Both art therapy and sandplay are considered creative art experiences, and the dynamics seen in one are often seen in the other. Landgarten has written, "The value of the art task is threefold: the *process* as a diagnostic, interactional, and rehearsal tool; the *contents* as a means of portraying unconscious and conscious communication; and the *product* as lasting evidence of the group's dynamics" (1987, p. 5, italics original). These apply directly to family sandplay as well as to family art therapy.

The content area in art therapy is the medium used and includes the size of the paper, pencils, markers, crayons, and so on. It might also include clay or pictures for collages. In sandplay, the content area is the patient's choice between wet and dry sand and the miniatures to be used. The process of family art therapy and family sandplay therapy are almost identical; the dynamics are revealed in the way the individuals go about building the scene together. The product or end result is the picture made or the scene produced. In sandplay, a photograph is taken to preserve the product, while in art therapy the picture itself is the product.

Both art therapy and sandplay can stimulate and nurture the creative process of the families involved.

> [I]n order to foster the sense of creative play with families, a strong connection to one's own inner child must also be maintained. It is inherent for the creative arts therapist, of course, but is a facet that the family therapist needs to nurture. It is only through our own creativity that we can bring hope and healing to the families with whom we come in contact. Our personal willingness to share in creative play can encourage families to look more deeply into their own resources, which can then enable them to handle future challenges more effectively. [Carey 1991, p. 239]

ເ໑ 3 ໑ະ

Equipping and Maintaining a Sandplay Office

A sandplay office can be a magical, unique setting, but the manner of its arrangement is dependent on the available space, combined with the personal interests of the sandplay therapist. There are advantages and disadvantages to every arrangement. Some therapists have the sandplay equipment as part of their interviewing office; others have a separate area. My sandplay room is separate from the main part of my office, with my waiting area located between the two rooms. In the past I have rented offices where the sandplay equipment was incorporated into the office space in a single room.

Ideally, the sandplay office should be large enough to provide sufficient shelf space to accommodate the miniatures in one's collection, along with an area for new toys as they are acquired. If one treats families in sandplay, adequate space must be allotted in order to avoid the sense of crowding when several persons are in the room.

Kalff's Sandplay room was unique. It was located in the downstairs area of her fourteenth-century farmhouse and had numerous nooks and crannies that held shelves packed full of every conceivable kind of miniature. Not many of us have such a wondrous collection.

EQUIPMENT

There should be two sand boxes available in the sandplay area, measuring 20" × 28" × 4". Each one is half-filled with sand and can be placed on a waist-high table (with attached wheels, if possible) (see Figure 3–1). One box contains dry sand and the other one wet sand. This can be diagnostically important because some patients are repelled by either the wet or the dry sand and this becomes an issue in treatment. The bottom of

Figure 3–1

the boxes should be painted with a blue waterproof paint, or lined with a blue waterproof backing similar to that used to line swimming pools. The reason for the blue color is that water or sky can be indicated when the sand is scooped out or pushed to one side. A waterproof base is a must, because water is frequently added to the box and such a base prevents leakage.

The above size was established by Dora Kalff because it enables one to view the entire contents of the tray without turning one's head from side to side. It is also a good size for photographing the scene. Most cameras will encompass this area. This size tray also provides a symbolic container for the expression of any number of thoughts and feelings, thereby limiting the scene to what the psyche can realistically handle at one time. These are the dimensions preferred by therapists who use a Jungian orientation. Other therapists have experimented with different sizes and shapes—oblong, circular, square, or round (see DeDomenico 1988).

I use two cameras as part of my equipment. What works best for me is a Polaroid and a fully automatic camera that is used for slides. If one is an accomplished camera person, it may be desirable to use another type of equipment. This is a personal preference.

The sand should half fill the boxes and should be sterilized to prevent any transmission of foreign organisms. The texture can range from coarse to very fine and should be of a natural color. Sandblasting sand, sometimes known as "sugar sand," is very fine and smooth; however, it may not be appropriate for very young children because they can get it into their eyes. Some therapists have used sand from the seashore, which contains tiny marine life. I would not recommend it. Others have experimented with different colors of sand. My feeling is that this gives an artificial tone to the work. Sand is sand and needs to be kept in its natural state.

The selection of miniatures should provide the patient with as large a choice as possible to portray his inner life. General categories are everything found in life and the imagination. They include all breeds of animals (prehistoric, wild and domestic), birds, vehicles (air, land, and sea), buildings, fences, bridges, trees, flowers, people in various occupations, cartoon figures, superheroes, doll house furniture, natural objects such as rocks, sea shells, pine cones, and feathers, and spiritual and religious items. The list could go on and on, the only limitations being available space and financial considerations. A part of my collection is seen in Figures 3–2 and 3–3.

One should never have anything in the collection that holds any kind of deep emotional significance for the therapist. Should the item accidentally break, the therapist might feel bad and this feeling could be transmitted to the maker. I have miniatures in two locations, with most of the items used by children in the Sandplay room. In my other, more formal office, there are two shelves where the breakable and expensive items are kept for use with adults and for training purposes. Several sources for buying Sandplay miniatures are listed in the Appendix. In addition to these sources, toy stores, flea markets, and garage sales are popular for collectors of miniatures.

Water is another necessity when one does Sandplay, both for moistening the sand and for cleanup purposes. It is a simple matter to dip the miniatures into a bucket of water before replacing them on the shelves. At times, however, water can be a nuisance, as when a patient wants to keep adding more

Figure 3–2

Figure 3–3

and more water, and the sand becomes sopping wet. I have had several children who flooded the box time after time, which made cleanup quite a task. I once had the opportunity to present such a case to Kalff. I have never forgotten her observation: "Don't forget to trust the process," a lesson well learned and often remembered. People have asked about limiting this type of flooding activity. I never do this, based on that one lesson of Kalff. If a child needs to flood, he needs to flood as long as he needs to flood. He will move beyond that stage when given the freedom to use the sand in his own unique way. This certainly creates a mess, and one should never undertake Sandplay if mess is intolerable. One learns how to do a relatively quick cleanup in these flooding instances (but don't expect the sand to dry out too quickly, as it takes water several days to evaporate from sand). For a quick cleanup a sponge, a bucket, and a turkey baster are essential but, most of all, what is needed is patience. The sand can be used for a relatively long time, but probably should be changed at least every three months.

The scene that is produced needs to be recorded in a way that can provide an ongoing record of the patient's process. I take two photographs, as mentioned earlier. One is a Polaroid picture that can be seen immediately; the other is a slide. I explain to the maker in advance that I will take photographs and I give the reason for this. I tell the child that the Polaroid pictures will be hers to keep at the end of therapy and the slides will be mine, so we will each have a record of the process. I also tell her during the initial session that the slides are sometimes used for teaching purposes. I make sure that I have permission from both the child and the parent to use the slides this way by asking that a release be signed (see Appendix). If for any reason permission is not granted, I take only the Polaroid pictures, which will ultimately be given to the child. I have found that providing the child with her Polaroid pictures is a positive way to terminate and the process becomes like a graduation experience. Some children have asked to take the Polaroid pictures home after the first or second one is taken. I remind them that this is not possible, and that we had agreed on the rules about this. This is one of the ways that a child tests me to determine if I mean what I say, and I share that observation with the child.

Other testing maneuvers that children often engage in, and some suggestions for addressing these issues are the following:

1. When a child asks to take a miniature home: This is usually discouraged, with the explanation that other children also use these toys and if everyone took one home each time, soon there would be no toys left. Sometimes it is helpful to go further and comment on the fact that the child would probably like to take a memento of this experience home, and that is understandable but impossible. Occasionally, the wish may be granted with a proviso that the toy be returned. This is done in cases where a child is in visible distress and needs the toy as a transitional object. One case that I recall was that of a boy with serious school issues. I felt that he needed to have this type of reminder during the week. The toy was always returned the following week. The requests continued for many months, until it became clear that the toy was no longer needed.

2. When a child steals a miniature: This is a delicate issue, because it is often not discovered until after the child has left. I have had a few such occasions. In one case, I chose to let it go initially, as the case was in a very tenuous stage. The child's mother had just died of AIDS and I found, after one session, that several dinosaurs were missing. I understood how very much the child needed to take a piece of this experience home with her and did not confront her at that time. A few weeks later, I introduced the subject by telling her that some of the dinosaurs were missing and wondered if she, too, had noticed this. She became quite defensive and finally told me that she had "borrowed" them. They were brought back the following week and became an integral part of her healing process.

3. When a child deliberately spills sand on the floor: I have seldom had this happen, but when it does I say that I wonder if he is testing me to see whether or not I will scold him. I tell him that the rules of therapy are different from those at home, but that I would appreciate it if he would try to keep the sand in the box. When a child is treated with respect in this way, he most often responds in kind. Several times I have had children say in the first interview, "What would you do if someone came in here and dumped the sand all over the floor?" My response is, "I guess I'd wonder what they were so angry about," and say that perhaps we should talk about it. I have never had a child actually overturn the sand box.

4. When a miniature is about to be destroyed: I usually intervene in these instances. I always tell a child dur-

ing the introductory stage that sometimes toys will fall on the floor and break and when this happens accidentally I will not feel bad because accidents do happen. However, I say that I will not allow the child to deliberately break a toy. When a toy is purposely broken, the child is expressing defiance of the rules. This may relieve his anger momentarily, but the relief is often followed by guilt. I do not want a broken toy to cause a child any more distress than he already feels. He needs to feel safe and to trust that I will stick to the rules, even if he does not.

5. When a child threatens to hit, spit, or kick: I firmly tell her this behavior is forbidden. I will not hit, kick, or spit at her and I expect the same sort of treatment. I will also attempt to help her link this behavior to the person or people she is really angry with, pointing out that I have not done anything to bring forth such anger. There are times when I have come quite close to being kicked. I try to remain calm and firm but nonpunitive. When these issues arise and are handled in an understanding, nonblaming way, the behavior is generally short-lived.

These guidelines for setting up and maintaining a sandplay office are general suggestions. The beauty of sandplay is that each therapist is free to use her own creativity in designing what works best for her. There are no hard and fast rules. Rather, there exists the wish to provide a healing space for the patients we are privileged to treat.

ᐧᑅ 4 ᗝᑊ

Beginning Treatment

Sandplay is a technique completely unknown to many people. For this reason one needs to pay special attention to how it is presented to patients if it is to be accepted as a credible treatment modality. The first section of this chapter discusses introducing the medium to parents at the initial interview. The second section focuses on introducing the medium to a child. The final section talks about how to present sandplay to a family.

Since parents are generally seen for a preliminary, factgathering session, Sandplay is discussed with them at that time. I usually ask the parents not to share this information with the child until he is brought to my office and can see it for himself. Often, however, the parent feels quite anxious about bringing the child for therapy, and will use the sand as an enticement. I recall one such situation: the case began as verbal therapy for the family; later it moved into individual Sandplay therapy for the two children; still later, family sessions were resumed. This was a highly verbal family of four, where each person tried to outtalk the other. The first few sessions were focused on an assessment of suicide risk in the 8-year-old daughter. She had threatened suicide by picking up a kitchen knife and saying that she might as well be dead. Because the initial sessions were of crisis proportions, it was deemed inappropriate to introduce Sandplay at that time. After the third or fourth session, when the tension level had decreased, I met with the parents to plan the next phase of treatment. My recommendation was that we discontinue the family sessions for a while, during which period each child would have some individual Sandplay therapy before family sessions were resumed at a later date. The reason for this decision lay in the dynamics of each child. The 8-year-old girl, the initial identified patient, had major issues related to depression and low self-esteem. The 6-year-old son was enuretic and encopretic resulting from his having endured a vicious attack by a dog when he was 3. Because the parents had serious problems with limit setting, it was agreed that they would be seen bi-weekly in parent counseling sessions. This family was not aware of the Sandplay room (since it is not in my main office) until I showed it to the parents. The children had started to rebel at family sessions when the treatment planning session was held with the parents, so that a transition to individual Sandplay therapy was appropriate. The parents used Sandplay as a bribe in order to get the children to return to therapy.

When I meet with parents for an initial interview or, as in this case, for goal setting, I show them the equipment and explain how I work and what they might expect. They are also told about the history and development of Sandplay and how it is used as a play therapy technique that addresses a wide category of diagnostic disorders.

I take parents into the Sandplay room and point out all the different categories of miniatures and some of the art materials that I use. Since some of my miniatures are in drawers, I pull those out for them to see as well. It is much more effective to do this than to simply talk about Sandplay.

Next, I cover all the confidentiality issues. I tell them this is the child's time, that he can tell them as much as he wants to, and that I will advise them if there are any major concerns. However, I ask that the parents refrain from asking the child details of the session. If a child wants to show his parent what he has done, I do allow that; however, I stress to the child and the parents that it is not required. The parents are informed that if they have any questions, they are free to call me and I will attempt to set their minds at ease. I tell them that photographs will be taken, and explain the reason for this. Parents are asked to sign a permission form during this session authorizing my use of the slides for teaching purposes (see Appendix).

Play therapy is also discussed with the parents because there is a common belief that "just playing" is not therapy. I have had several parents tell me they will get a sandbox so that the child can do this at home. A great deal of time is spent explaining to parents that play therapy requires expertise in many different areas, such as the ages and stages of child development, family developmental stages, and how I see their child benefiting from therapeutic intervention, given the presenting problem. If time permits, I offer some insights into other aspects of the play therapy process, such as the metaphoric, symbolic nature of play, pointing out that children are naturally equipped to think in metaphors, which are far easier for them than analytical thinking.

Parents are told that although I am always available to them by phone, I will not reveal to them anything that the child has told me in confidence unless there is a significant risk of harm involved. Sometimes, after a child has shown a parent her sand picture, the parent will call, wanting me to interpret it for her. I try very hard to explain the picture in general terms, without revealing the underlying dynamics. For example, one mother saw her daughter's sand picture containing on one side a threatening dragon on top of a castle; on the other side, a girl and two dogs were sitting. The dragon appeared quite threatening. The mother asked me if this was how her daughter saw her. I said that might have been part of the scene, but that the picture probably represented much more than that. This explanation was offered in order to allow the mother to have some input into the process and to confirm her view without my agreeing that the child saw her as a dragon, which was only one aspect of the situation.

Some parents will spend an inordinate amount of time looking at their child's picture in an attempt to understand it from a thinking perspective. When this happens, I repeat that Sandplay is a *process* and that the end product is to be viewed symbolically.

Presenting Sandplay to a child is generally an easy procedure, since sand and play are so universally accepted by children. Many children exhibit unbounded enthusiasm and will quickly take the nearest toys and put them into one sand box or the other, demonstrating very little selectivity. This is expected the first time or two a child comes. I spend the initial session with a child trying to help her feel comfortable by not limiting her exploration in any way. I talk while the child explores the toys and other equipment and explain to her that the scenes she produces will help me understand how she feels. I also tell her some of the information the parent gave me before I met her, although I avoid any delicate areas at this time. I explain that words do not always let adults know what a child needs, but that it is possible, through Sandplay, for her to show me how she feels, rather than having to tell me.

The confidentiality issues are also discussed. The child is told that she is free to tell her parent whatever she wants about what she has done with me and that she also has the right *not* to tell the parent, if she so chooses. Most children are surprised by this and somewhat relieved to learn that they can have this kind of special relationship with an adult, without involving a parent.

The child is told that I will not tell the parent anything that she has revealed to me in confidence, unless I think she might be in some sort of danger. I assure her, however, I will always let her know in advance what might be said to a parent and when, should such a situation ever arise. Further, she will be free to be present when I discuss such a matter with the parent. This is the case if there is any suspicion of physical or sexual abuse, as it is imperative that the parent be made aware of these issues. If the authorities need to be involved, the child is told that as well.

The issue of safety is discussed, that is, that the child is not allowed to hurt himself or me, and that the toys are not to be deliberately broken. (If one is accidentally broken during use, the child will not be reprimanded.) One other safety issue that I impose is related to my dangerous driveway. I tell the child that he cannot leave the waiting room without a parent. This is especially vital with younger children.

Depending on their age, children are advised of the time constraints of therapy. Very young children (under 6 or 7), who have no conception of time, are told that they will be given a few minutes' notice before the session ends. Older children, as they learn to tell time, can see for themselves the clock on the wall, but I also give the older child a five-minute warning before the end of the session.

Occasionally one encounters a child who finds sand threatening. This is very evident from the child's behavior and the therapist can comment on it. He could say, for example, that it seems as if the child might not want to get his hands dirty. This gives him a realistic defense against what might be too threatening at the moment. He is then reassured that he is not obligated to play in the sand, but it is there if he would like to. If he chooses not to use the sand, he is offered an alternative, such as drawing, painting, or clay. This is one cardinal rule: Sandplay is never pushed if there is overt resistance.

After a family and/or child has been assessed for a treatment recommendation, the decision may be to use family sandplay therapy. Since the original introduction to Sandplay has already occurred, the parents have a beginning familiarity with the medium. Additionally, however, they are told that, by participating in this kind of play with their children, they may discover different ways of relating as a family. It is especially useful to point this out when the family is either highly verbal or argumentative. In such cases it is explained that words are not always necessary in order to get a message across, that in fact sometimes words are more of a hindrance than a help.

It is often helpful to begin family sandplay by having the members construct a scene together without speaking. When it has been completed, the reaction is usually one of wonderment that so much has been revealed without the spoken word. Discussion does take place near the conclusion of each session, so the experience can be assimilated. The recommended way to accomplish this phase is to have each family member talk about his or her contribution to the overall scene, what he can observe about his part and how it relates to the other parts. The therapist withholds any observations until all the family members have presented their views, and very little interpretation is offered until the family structure has been strengthened. In the early stages it is best to listen, to observe, and to make mental notes for use when the timing is more appropriate. The reason for this is that if a therapist is too eager to offer interpretations, the family process is interrupted and foreshortened. Families will come to their own resolutions, given the required time and support.

Some possible ways to structure the sessions are:

1. Have family members choose teams. One team is instructed to make a sand picture in the wet sand box, the other team to do the same in the dry. When the family members select teams themselves, the present alliances within the family are illustrated. The therapist can then structure the following sessions, using different teams in order to begin to alter the relationships. This is especially valuable when it is obvious to the therapist that the existing alliances are unhealthy ones.

2. One person can make the scene while the others are silent observers. A discussion can then be held, allowing each person to contribute his comments.

3. The therapist may wish to structure a session by telling family members that they are not to talk to each other but they are to make a scene without speaking . This is a useful technique for families who are argumentative or overly verbal.
4. On the other hand, the therapist may wish to structure a session by instructing family members to talk about what they are going to do. This technique is useful for families who do not appear to interact with each other or for those with limited verbal skills.

Therapists are encouraged to experiment with these approaches or else to use their own creativity in designing others. There are no absolutes in this work, no hard and fast rules, only a willingness to use the materials in a respectful, therapeutic framework that will enhance the communication patterns of the family patient.

᪥ 5 ᪥

Examples of Individual Sandplay Therapy

This chapter illustrates the use of Sandplay with individual children. It is divided into two sections. The first part is a full case presentation, with representative stages from different phases of the child's therapy. The second part offers examples of cases from different diagnostic categories and varied age groups of boys and girls. It is important to note that the pictures that have been selected are offered simply as samples of the many ways in which children express themselves. They are not meant to be seen as the only possible visual representation of a given situation.

PRISCILLA

Priscilla was 6 years old when her mother was struck and killed by a car. She was the only child of her parents, although a half-brother from the mother's previous marriage had also lived with the family. Almost immediately after the mother's death, the boy was sent to live with his natural father. Priscilla continued to live with her father, and every day after school her paternal grandmother cared for her. Priscilla and her father usually had dinner at her grandmother's house. After dinner, she was given the choice of where to spend the night: she could go home with Dad or she could stay with her grandmother, which she frequently did.

Priscilla was in kindergarten at the time of her mother's death. The adults in her family and her teachers were concerned that she showed no reaction to the death until a year later, when she became quite aggressive towards other children. This initial lack of affect illustrates how some young children deal with death. They can only manage such a huge trauma in small bits and pieces. This can seem like denial to adults, but it means simply that the child's psyche can only deal with loss in minimal amounts at any given time.

Nancy Boyd Webb (1993) has outlined the considerations that differentiate the grief of children from that of adults:

1. Children's immature cognitive development, which interferes with understanding about the irreversibility, universality, and inevitability of death.
2. Children's limited capacity to tolerate emotional pain.
3. Children's limited ability to verbalize their feelings.
4. Children's sensitivity about "being different" than their peers. [p. 14]

All of these limitations were seen in Priscilla. At age 6, she was unclear about the finality and irreversibility of death, had very little tolerance for emotional pain, had extreme difficulty in expressing feelings, and was quite sensitive about "being different."

The first time that I saw Priscilla I found her very open and receptive, a most charming little girl. Her first sand picture (Figure 5–1) was one in which she carefully lined up just about every animal she could find. This scene was constructed in the wet sand box. After completing it, she moved to the dry sand box and used giraffes with people watching them (Figure 5–2). The giraffe, with its long neck, is often interpreted as symbolizing an attempt to "stay above it all" in order to avoid the turmoil that is going on down below. Her choice of a giraffe expressed Priscilla's attempt to control her anxiety, while at the same time she was examining the toys that were available.

During the construction of this scene Priscilla and I began to get acquainted. I told her how sorry I was about her mother's

Figure 5–1

Figure 5–2

death. She replied that it was made even worse because she had also lost her brother, which was her allusion to the fact that he was now living with his natural father. This may have been an attempt to minimize the loss of her mother. However, it was clear that she felt both losses acutely.

The following week Priscilla reported a dream: "I was on a bridge and the bridge broke and I fell in the water and drowned. I woke up screaming and crying." This frightening dream was undoubtedly related to the loss of her mother and could be interpreted as a suicidal fantasy, a means of joining her lost parent—a dynamic often seen in children who have experienced a major loss. The dream also illustrated and confirmed that she was suffering from Post-Traumatic Stress Disorder (*DSM-IV* 1994). I did not discuss the dream with her during this session because it was only the second time that I had seen this child. I made a mental note of it, however.

Priscilla made two more scenes in the sand during the following session. The first was an illustration of a zoo, as she was about to go there on a class trip. The construction of the scene of an impending happy event can be interpreted as a demonstration of denial, with a focus on the present rather than the past. There were also two treasure boxes in this scene, and a bridge with two babies on top (which may have been her way of including aspects of the preceding dream). There were also two mothers seated on steps, a boat, two organs, two pterodactyls, a huge cobra, and a turtle. The use of so many twos is often for the purpose of highlighting a situation. In this case, it could have indicated her wish to reunite, not only with her mother but also with her brother.

The second scene contained figures from *Aladdin* and *Beauty and the Beast*, two of her favorite movies. This was a continued attempt for her to stay in the present. She also put some figures inside of tepees, which represented a safe place for her. The tepee, a place of home and hearth, is often illustrative of the security of home. There are also two dinosaur skeletons fighting, which illustrated her unconscious angry feelings about Mom's death. A volcano that is about to erupt over everyone is also in this scene, an illustration of just how vulnerable and angry she felt. With this scene Priscilla, at last, had begun to express her rage over her mother's death.

Two weeks after the bridge dream, Priscilla told me of another dream. She and Mom were in a car. There was an accident and Mom was killed. This dream woke her up and she spent the rest of that night with her father. The dream was further corroboration that she was, indeed, suffering from Post-

Traumatic Stress syndrome. Again, Priscilla made two sand pictures during the session. Traumatized children often need to make two scenes because of the enormity of their experience.

The first scene Priscilla constructed was that of a hospital, and might have expressed her attempt at a resolution of this frightening dream. However, her mother had been a nurse's aide and occasionally took Priscilla to work with her. The scene might have represented several things for Priscilla: in it both the mothers and the babies were patients; placing them in a hospital setting ensured that help was being provided for them. Hospital equipment, when used in Sandplay, often represents the child's unconscious understanding that the Sandplay office is a place of healing. In this example, the scene of the hospital equipment might also have helped Priscilla remember happy experiences she had shared with Mom. Happy memories are necessary, if a positive grief resolution is to occur.

The second sandbox contained a scene of feeding, which illustrated that Priscilla was experiencing nurturance in this setting. Two ladybugs sat on a table and several eggs were in view. Trees, a cave, and a ladder were also there. Priscilla took great care with one central egg, which appeared to be her ego/ Self representation. She positioned this egg in center stage, which affirmed to me that she was now in a positive, more age-appropriate stage. This picture was produced after four months of therapy and is an example of how quickly Sandplay can reach some inner repressed material.

During the next couple of weeks Priscilla appeared quite anxious, and flitted from one thing to another. She would begin a sand picture, decide to completely change it, then decide to abandon the project altogether. It is possible that the level reached during her previous Sandplay session sent her once again into a period of denial. This is a frequent occurrence in Sandplay. When there is an uncovering of significant material, it can be followed by an attempt at repression. During this period of anxiety, she did not produce any sand pictures. Instead, she painted or we played therapeutic games.

The next sand scene Priscilla made came after six months of therapy and was reminiscent of the chaos evident in her first sand picture, especially in the use of a large number of pigs. She used all the pigs in my collection, all the dogs, and all the rabbits, placing them in no particular order. I saw this as a regressive phase, which is necessary in the overall healing of the psyche.

The story of Demeter and Persephone in Greek mythology seems applicable to Priscilla's situation. This myth symbolizes a lost mother–daughter connection. One day, in the little town of Eleusis, the young Persephone was playing with her friends when suddenly the earth opened up and she was snatched into the underworld by Hades. Demeter, her mother, heard Persephone's screams and tried to run after her. However, just as Demeter was about to reach her daughter, the ground opened up and swallowed Persephone. Demeter's pigs, however, quickly ran ahead of her and were able to get down through the opening in the ground before Demeter got to the site.

Much later in time, rites were developed that celebrated the reunion of Persephone and Demeter (Meter=Mater=Great Mother). These became known as the Eleusinian Mysteries. They were held at Eleusis at the site where Persephone supposedly disappeared. During these rites, the initiates to the mysteries would descend singly to the sea, each bearing a suckling piglet for purification and sacrifice. The pig was offered as a sacrificial animal, symbolizing the lost mother–daughter connection (Parke 1977).

The next scene Priscilla made in that session was a zoo, with a leopard emerging from an igloo. The igloo is a cold home, and it might have illustrated the emptiness this child felt at the loss of her mother. The leopard might have represented a re-emergence of her anger. Priscilla also placed marbles in a treasure chest. Marbles, when used this way, are often symbolic of inner treasure. She was now feeling that she had an inner treasure, in spite of the elements in the rest of the scene that indicated a sense of emptiness and anger. I had recently added a casket to my collection, which Priscilla found. She placed a raccoon in it and carefully added a funeral scene in one corner of the box. She carefully buried the casket and placed a tombstone at its head. This was a most symbolic burial and one that helped her to proceed with her grieving in a more conscious way.

The following session found Priscilla's scene (Figure 5–3) to be quite different from any she had made before. She positioned many things around the edge of the dry sand and cleared a central spot for water, boats with sun bathers, octopi, and fish. On one shore sat a large rat and a coiled snake. On the right, were two *very* large ants, and in the upper right corner one *very* tiny Barbie doll. Such a tiny figure often represents how small and powerless the person feels, which would be the case with this Barbie as she faced those very large insects. For Priscilla (as Barbie), it expressed her feeling of powerlessness to defend herself against the frightening ants, rat, and snake. The scene represented her continuing struggle to face the loss of her mother and her brother.

A carnival scene with snakes was depicted in the other box. Priscilla talked about the bike rider in this scene, who didn't watch where he was going. He did a flip-flop and hurt himself.

Figure 5–3

I commented that he needed to be careful and watch where he was going, and perhaps that was something like what happened to her mother (who was killed stepping off a curb). Priscilla was quick to say, in Mom's defense, that it was dark and Mom couldn't see. I said that it was probably more likely that the driver of the car couldn't see.

Priscilla's next sand picture (Figure 5–4) came after a summer break and showed a definite move forward. In this scene she used giraffes, dogs, zebras, a red bird sitting on eggs, a large deer, a car getting gasoline, and a few other assorted items. All the animals were in a circular/mandala formation, with four tiny kittens nestled in the center. This picture is a nice example of the Constellation of the Self. The animals are all observing the births of the new kittens, symbolic of her own rebirth. The bird with the eggs carries out the same theme. The car being

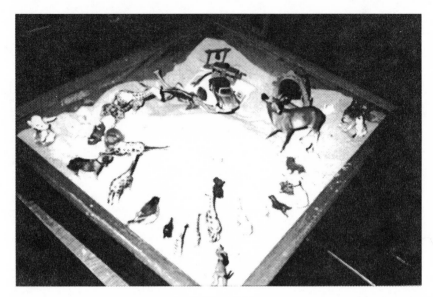

Figure 5–4

filled with gasoline is symbolic of new energy. This picture was made after seven months of therapy. She was now able to express her feelings about missing her mother and her brother.

Figure 5–5 showed evidence of movement into a new phase of treatment. This scene depicts a farm with all of the various species of animals contained within their own boundaries. Note the large number of pigs, once again. The piglets in this picture are separated from their mothers. As a metaphoric way of recognizing her feelings, I said to Priscilla that the piglets must have felt very lost and abandoned. She made no comment about this, but appeared quite solemn.

For several months, Priscilla and I played many therapeutic games that were designed to enhance communication and that allowed her to express her negative self-image. On one occasion she formed her hand into a fist and pointed one finger, which resembled a gun, towards her face, saying that she hated her face. She then symbolically blasted it away. I found this to be very upsetting, but I explored the issue with her. I explained that when a parent has died a child feels very bad about herself and has thoughts that she might like to join the dead parent. I also explained that this sometimes meant that a child saw herself as ugly or less desirable than other children, but that this was not the case with her at all. I stressed that she had many fine strengths, that she was not ugly, and that she had a positive future to look towards. She seemed reassured, and there was never another incident like this.

Priscilla made the next two scenes a few weeks later. In the dry sand box she placed Aladdin, the Beast, and a couple of babies who were about to drown. In the wet sand box (Figure 5–6), she constructed an Indian scene with tepees and a

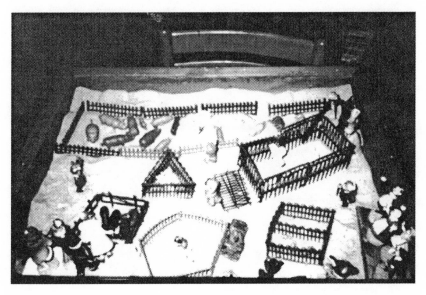

Figure 5–5

wishing well that had a large round marble in the center. She made a circular enclosure with marbles for the wishing well. Jasmine sat on the ancient columns, and her tiger approached. There were trees and plants as well. In this scene Priscilla continued to work on her mourning process. The first scene demonstrated babies about to drown, whereas the second scene was filled with hope and growth.

The therapeutic work continued with the next scene Priscilla made. It was another reworking of the mother/baby/pig theme and expressed her continued attempts to compartmentalize her grief. By now she was less focused on her loss and did not appear to be as visibly depressed.

Priscilla had begun to dislike school and there was some question about a learning disability, so I arranged for her to

Figure 5–6

have an independent psychological evaluation. The psychologist ascertained that as the school work became more advanced, Priscilla might experience increased frustration. Some mathematical concepts had become quite difficult for her and she also evidenced serious expressive difficulties. Her grandmother shared the evaluation with Priscilla's school, which led to her receiving appropriate supplemental help. This resulted in a significant improvement in Priscilla's school functioning.

The following year Priscilla entered a school that was near her grandmother's house, making the after-school hours easier on everyone. Not long after her entrance to this school, the next scene (Figure 5–7) was produced. This scene again contains the pigs, which are carefully enclosed, as are the sheep (to the left), and dogs and cats (to the right). The horses were allowed

Figure 5–7

to run free, which expressed the freedom she was then feeling. The top portion of this scene held special interest. A solid house stands with a bridge next to it, and a family in front of the bridge. The bridge was reminiscent of Priscilla's early dream and the mother is shown with the family, but the mother figure is lying down. This illustrated that her mother's presence was felt, but that the death had altered the situation. Priscilla had not forgotten her mother, but had recognized the limitations related to her loss.

The latter stages of a child's therapy often reveal her interest in day-to-day events, the stage that Neumann (1973) termed *adaptation to the collective* (also known as the solar-rational stage). The Lion King became Priscilla's favorite story and for many weeks she set up a scene similar to Figure 5–8

Figure 5–8

and made up her own version of the story. She was now able to verbalize her thoughts and feelings more effectively. The story she told about this picture was that all the animals (the collection in the center) had gone to find the Lion King (in the upper left corner). They met other lions on the way who tried to prevent them from going on. However, the animals were victorious in the end. This story was illustrative of the problems she had overcome in our work together.

The next scene contained three parts. First, in the sand was what Priscilla called a "traffic jam" (Figure 5–9). Cars were lined up in opposite directions and placed between houses on either side. On top of the other sand box she placed the doll house. She said this was the second part of the scene. Last, there was a hospital scene off to one side. The story she told was about

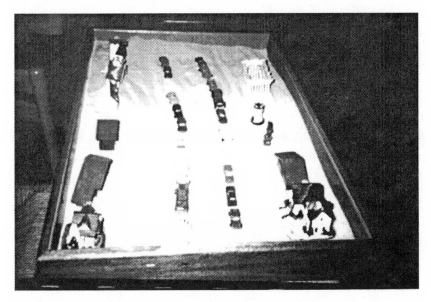

Figure 5–9

a new house where the baby got tossed out by the girl. This was in response to the fact that Priscilla's cousin had a new baby sister and had just moved into a new house. Priscilla and her cousin had a sibling-like relationship; the grandmother cared for both of them after school, so the advent of another child into the family brought up intense feelings of rivalry. She was also envious of the fact that her cousin had a complete family and a new house, two things that were not available to her.

Termination was being considered when another trauma struck this family. Priscilla's father had a very serious injury at work and it took many months before anyone knew how permanently disabling his condition might be. Fortunately, he did recover after a couple of surgical procedures. This entire episode, however, brought up anew Priscilla's fears of abandonment by her only remaining parent. Additionally, the accident made her father even more depressed than he had been and left him with very little available energy. Priscilla's grandmother, also, was placed under further stress by this turn of events. She was concerned not only about the effects on Priscilla, but also the very real situation of whether or not her son would ever be able to function in his work or as a parent.

Priscilla rallied quite well after the initial shock of Dad's accident and she did well in school that year. She was, eventually, a happy little 9-year-old girl who was developing like most children her age. When termination drew near, I scheduled sessions every other week in order to continue our relationship on a less frequent basis. This frequency was decided upon in order to address her abandonment fears in relation to me. Priscilla herself decided after several months of the lessened frequency that she was ready to give up therapy. Her family was advised that there might be future periods when she would benefit from additional support, such as when she entered puberty, or if any more unexpected events or losses were to occur.

Many aspects of this case were addressed through a child-centered approach to Sandplay therapy. At the beginning of treatment Priscilla was in shock and denial. She progressed through the mourning process with periods of anger, grief, sadness, and fear, eventually attaining resolution. These same stages had to be re-addressed in relation to her father's accident. It is hoped that the selected pictures from this case have illustrated some of the work that was accomplished.

DIAGNOSTIC EXAMPLES

The following pictures are presented to show work that was done with patients from different diagnostic categories. Again, it must be stressed that these are not provided as the only ways in which certain situations might be expressed through Sandplay, that they are only some examples among many possibilities. Please note that all of the following pictorial examples represent but one single moment in the overall treatment process.

Divorce

Children of divorce present themselves in a variety of ways, dependent on many factors. First is the child's individual adjustment capacity, which has been prefigured by his original personality style and the parenting he experienced up to the point of divorce. Some children have minimal adjustment issues while certain others may have more difficult scenarios. It appears that a child who is by nature more robust and outgoing will experience less trauma than a child who is more sensitive. (This is a very broad generalization, and the situation may reflect the fact that children for whom therapy is sought are skewed samples.) The more sensitive a child is, the more likely he will need therapy, whether there is a divorce issue or not.

Some of the symptoms that bring a child of divorce into treatment are stomachaches, headaches, poor sleep patterns, nightmares, night terrors, separation anxiety, school phobia, a significant drop in school performance, and aggression towards peers and/or adults. Many of these issues are revealed by anxiety and depressive symptoms.

Anxiety

This picture (Figure 5–10) was the first one produced by an extremely anxious 6-year-old girl. She exhibited major anxiety symptoms following her parents' separation. She felt (as do many other children) that her father no longer loved her "or else he wouldn't have gone away." The scene reveals the child's feeling that she was split right through the center. On either side is a beach scene, with shells and rocks on both sides. On the upper half of the scene are trees and flowering shrubs; on the lower side the shells form a circle, with some birds and a kitten in the center. In the water area are two more shells and a flowering shrub.

In an attempt to understand the meaning in this first picture, the three items in the center might be interpreted as her attempt to bring her parents back together. While the two sides of the scene are separated, each side has its own unique qual-

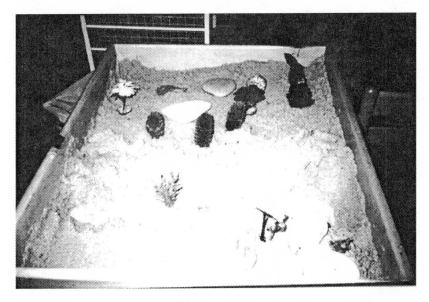

Figure 5–10

ity. The upper portion has growth and a centering movement around the white shell. The shell is a strong feminine symbol since it is found in the depths of the ocean, which is the realm of the feminine. The lower half of the scene contains a sand dollar, which is sometimes viewed as a symbol of the Self. A bird and a kitten are also there. Birds are seen as carriers of the spirit because they fly between heaven and earth, while a kitten represents a small feminine being.

While this child was undoubtedly suffering a great deal at that time, I believed the prognosis to be positive because of the many signs in her picture that indicated centering, growth, and spirituality. She showed that her parenting experiences had been positive up to this period, even though she also had a sensitive nature. These signs are not always evident at such an early period in therapy.

The next picture is an example of anxiety in an 8-year-old boy in the early stage of therapy. A new baby brother had come into the house. Figure 5–11 illustrates a typical anxiety reaction. The boy has contrived all sorts of things that refer to his anxiety: a dragon and space capsule are flying overhead, and a large quantity of miniatures is used. I interpreted the bridge as his attempt to rise above the chaos. The large crocodile and part of the bridge extend beyond the perimeter. One can feel the boy's anxiety in such a picture. He was suffering extreme fear as to how the advent of a new child would affect his place in the family.

Depression

This scene (Figure 5–12) is by a 9-year-old boy who had been in therapy more than a year. He came from a highly dysfunc-

Figure 5–11

Figure 5–12

tional family with drug and alcohol issues. During much of the time that I treated him, his father was in a rehabilitation program. He and his mother lived in her parents' dysfunctional home. The boy shared his mother's bed and had numerous issues, such as the need for appropriate boundaries, castration anxiety, poor school performance, separation anxiety, and nightmares.

The picture shows his attempt to resolve some of these concerns. The fences were his way of illustrating the need for boundaries. However, they were not yet efficient, because they were totally unconnected at this stage. In the top portion of the picture (difficult to see) is an underground tunnel, with a man who is carrying a gun. Another man is crouched down, almost out of sight. The phallic implication of the gun was not to be overlooked. R2D2 of *Star Wars* is swimming towards the men, and might have illustrated the child's feeling of alienation from his peers. He was also a frequent daydreamer at school. The cave in the foreground is where he had stashed what he called "treasure." Buried treasure was a frequent theme for this young boy. Sometimes it was quite visible, sometimes hidden, but almost always present in his scenes.

Given the family history, this child's future was always in doubt prognostically, but through therapy he became increasingly aware that he had an inner treasure. He needed much stronger protection for the treasure, however, than the fences illustrated in this scene.

This next construction (Figure 5–13), produced by an 8-year-old girl, was made on top of the sand box and clearly spoke to her suicidal thoughts. She began the scene by building the log cabin, then proceeded to add the miniatures. The adults are unconcerned as they sit on a bench with their backs to the children. One child is poised to jump from the roof. Another child is inside, looking out. This patient was in the midst of a chaotic family situation with drug, alcohol, and divorce issues, and in this picture she was making certain that her feelings were known.

Adjustment Reactions

Adjustment reactions are generally caused by some disequilibrium in the child's family, such as the move to a new area; a change of school; the separation of parents; the hospitalization of the child, a sibling, or a parent; the death of a significant relative; an automobile accident; or the witnessing of a traumatic event. The causes are varied and bring varied re-

Figure 5–13

sponses. Some typical reactions run the gamut of symptom-atology: anxiety, depression, poor school performance, aggressiveness towards peers or authority figures, stealing, enuresis, encopresis. The reactions in older children and adolescents can have more serious consequences and might include such things as drug and/or alcohol experimentation, running away from home, sexual acting out, or criminal activity.

Figure 5–14 was made by a boy of 4 who exhibited serious aggressive acting-out episodes. He was in danger of being expelled from nursery school because he had thrown sand at his teacher on the playground. The child came from an intact family, although one with a history of paternal alcoholism and violent parental arguments. This example of his Sandplay was executed after about six months of therapy. The

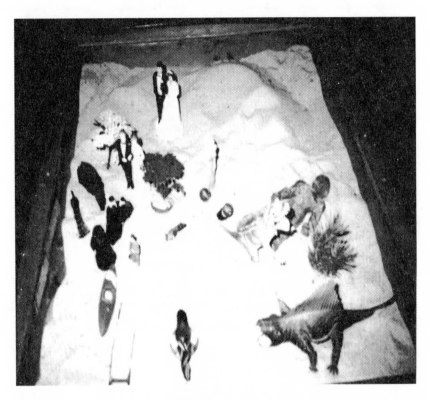

Figure 5–14

predominant features are the two dinosaurs with open mouths, one who has felled the Hulk. These figures reveal the boy's anger. There are also two brides and grooms. One pair has a couple of rockets nearby. These brides and grooms represented his wish for his parents to make peace; the rockets, however, made this seem unlikely. The wounded soldier (standing near the litter) has evidently recovered; he represented the child's state at the time. Also included were a red bird and three flowering trees, welcome sights, to me—symbols of growth in the midst of turmoil.

Sexual Abuse

The issue of sexual abuse of children is difficult to assess. In cases where there has been disclosure, it is more accessible to intervention. In other cases, denial can be so strong that there is total repression of any memory of the event. Dissociation can exist in both situations. An example of each type of case follows.

This profound picture (Figure 5–15), made by an 11-year-old boy, is a graphic depiction of what he would like to do as retribution for the sexual abuse he suffered for four years. The perpetrator was his uncle. He had internalized the edict "don't tell" and almost his entire therapy was nonverbal and quite poignant; he seldom spoke a word. I attempted to verbalize for him what he might be feeling, and he would nod either yes or no to what I had suggested. In this scene, he has constructed a jail for the perpetrator made of popsicle sticks. Inside is the burned figure of a soldier (a miniature he had burned under supervision during a previous session). The burned figure could represent both the perpetrator and how damaged this boy felt. Nearby stand a car and a bicycle, possible signs of his hope of escape. I was recently advised by the referring therapist of this boy that his family had moved to the South, that the boy was an honor student, and that he had a girlfriend. The only therapy this child experienced was Sandplay and the therapy was primarily nonverbal.

A 5-year-old girl who lived with both parents and who was ritually abused by her grandparents made this scene. She was also molested by a babysitter. None of this had been disclosed at

Figure 5–15

the time that she made Figure 5–16, which shows giraffes, one in a box, two adults on a bed, a smaller one on another bed, an even smaller one on a hospital bed. She frequently placed a giraffe in a boxlike structure and in this way illustrated the burial motif that was part of the grisly ritual. The small giraffe placed on a bed probably represented the babysitter's molestation as well as that of the grandparents. The giraffe in the hospital bed could have been her hope of being healed in therapy. The use of giraffes, in the same way as that noted in an earlier case, was symbolic of her meager attempts to stay above the conflict. I believe the giraffe may have also symbolized her dissociation. The hopeful sign I found in this picture was the butterfly on top of the house. The butterfly is a symbol of transformation and, while it is quite fragile, it is nonetheless present.

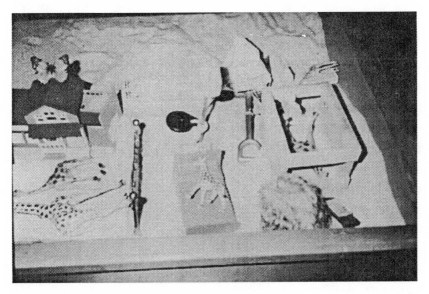

Figure 5–16

Learning Disabilities

The learning-disabled child has unique issues, which may be compounded by situational factors as well. The learning-disabled child, almost without exception, exhibits a poor self-image, has low self-esteem, and feels stupid and unliked. He gives up trying or becomes belligerent. His history of poor school performance goes back at least to kindergarten. The fortunate child is the one who is diagnosed early enough so that appropriate interventions can be made. However, many of these children are not assessed until extremely poor organizational skills have developed and they begin to lag ever further behind their peers. The emotional overlay stemming from learning disabilities is a challenge to every therapist.

Parental education is a must for these children and needs to be built into the treatment plan.

Figure 5–17 was made by a learning-disabled 10-year-old girl whose mother had fought the school for several years to obtain appropriate services for her. The child managed to just get by until she became preadolescent. At that time she was tested and placed in a special education program where she was finally able to assimilate the curriculum. Therapy was instituted, ostensibly not because of the learning disability but because of her depression over the death of her grandfather. It was conceivable that this shock (her grandfather's death) was the event that helped her begin to deal with her issues of low self-esteem and poor self-image. The picture was made when she

Figure 5–17

was 11½, near the time of termination. It is an orderly picture and one that holds great promise for the future. There is a split down the middle of the scene, but a bridge that goes over the river connects the two sides. The river needs to be crossed in order to get to the wedding and the wishing well, and the bridge enables her to do this. Her joy is evident in the ferris wheel, a symbol of childhood. Penguins, dressed in their tuxedos, follow the bride and groom toward the wedding scene. This picture affirms that she was actively entering the transition from childhood to adolescence with a strong sense of her own self-worth.

The next case example is that of a boy who was 6 years old when he came to therapy. In addition to the diagnosis of Attention Deficit Hyperactive Disorder, this child had numerous other problems. His father died when he was merely 8 months old and his mother was left with two very young children to raise. The boy was diagnosed quite early as developmentally delayed and showed signs of Obsessive-Compulsive Disorder as well. He was placed in a special preschool setting. When the problems continued, he was assessed by a pediatric neurologist and additionally diagnosed with Tourette's Syndrome. He had been on trial periods of numerous medications until the correct combination was arrived at. These diagnoses were all made by the time he was 6 years old. He was fortunate to have had a very knowledgeable mother, one who sought out the best for her son every step of the way. He was brought to therapy because he expressed a long-delayed reaction to his father's death. As one can surmise from this extensive history, there were many additional problems.

Sand was initially quite difficult for this boy to tolerate because of his obsessive-compulsive symptoms, but slowly he began to be more comfortable with it. I have chosen two examples because of the numerous dynamics of this case. Figure 5–18 was produced near the end of his first year of therapy. In this picture he managed to partially contain the dinosaurs, which represented his unconscious rage at the loss of his father as well as at his handicapped condition, which was accompanied by many fears and obsessions. The reader can see the obsessive qualities in the way the trees, the motorized vehicles, and the cowboys on horseback are lined up. The scene took him a full hour to construct because of his obsessive attention to each detail, with constant arranging and rearranging of the miniatures. The presence of trees and

Figure 5–18

motorized vehicles was a positive indication to me that growth was now occurring and that there was energy available for the task.

Figure 5–19 was made almost three years later. In this scene the trucks are in a position similar to that in the previous scene. However, there is less rage present and workmen stand nearby. The dinosaurs have been replaced by lions and other zoo animals, all of them well secured in their cages. The addition of more human figures shows progress as well. The work trucks represent positive energy for him, and a workman wheels a wheelbarrow. He also has placed some superhero figures and their weapons along one side. These represent his inner protectors that, by now, were in place. In the center is a rabbit hutch with bunnies in it. Two organs are nearby. The bunnies

Figure 5–19

are his expression of a developing anima connection and the organs are indicative of his spirituality.

Oppositional Disorder

The child with this symptomatology is one who has severe relationship problems. This is a difficult child for parents and teachers alike, one who has either no peer relationships or very poor ones. Two examples follow.

About four months after starting therapy, a very oppositional boy of 8 made Figure 5–20. He used red paper to construct this volcano with lava pouring over the sides. The dinosaurs represent much of his rage as they try to ascend the mountain while, at the same time, they are being threatened by the volcanic overflow.

Figure 5–20

A 9-year-old girl illustrated the story of her life with Figure 5–21. The presenting symptom was oppositionalism. She explained that the family in the center had all been killed as Santa rode by on his sleigh. She uses cotton for the heavenly clouds on which the dead family floats as Santa delivers his goods. On the ground is a town with people going to church to pray. Other people merely sit and watch. The reason for the intensity of her rage was discovered only later: she was being molested by her father. The symptom of oppositionalism was a direct result of her unspoken rage. The dead family in the scene represented her killing rage against the man who had violated her and the mother who had not protected her. I might add that in several cases such as this, cotton has been used in various ways. The intent seems to be to provide a protective cover for the psyche of the child.

Figure 5–21

Visually Impaired

This next picture (Figure 5–22) was made by a child who was legally blind. This caused her much anguish as she sought desperately to keep up with her peers and to compensate for her handicap. Her sessions were focused on helping improve her shaky self-esteem. She took a great deal of time in constructing her scenes, as she had to study each figure intently in order to ascertain what it was. In this Sandplay picture she constructed a sand castle in the foreground before adding the figures. Her rage was expressed through the use of as many dragons as she could find. The spiders were symbolic of how "creepy" she felt. This was produced about halfway through her therapy, which lasted for almost a year.

Figure 5–22

Speech Problem

Sandplay is a natural for children when speech is either delayed or incomprehensible. Expression is made possible through the use of sand and miniatures.

This scene (Figure 5–23) was made by a child of 5 who was very difficult to understand when he began the therapeutic process. It illustrates how he felt about himself and was made about three months into treatment. The soldiers and dinosaurs symbolize his inner battles with self-expression. He also placed bombs and rockets, set to go off. He made many similar scenes, where he and I had intense battles—that he always won.

Figure 5–23

Birthmark

The child who is born with any kind of obvious deformity or marking can never escape the notice of others. Birthmarks come from a variety of causes. Some are genetic, some are birth accidents, some are unexplained. Whatever the cause, the effects last for life. Children such as these need much nurturance and much care.

An 8-year-old girl who had a port wine stain that covered more than 50 percent of her body made many scenes of feeding as she struggled against great odds to feel normal. Her major solace was food, which she illustrated in many of her sand pictures. In Figure 5–24, she took great care to set an elegant table, using items from the doll house. Then she added many

Figure 5–24

figures to partake of the banquet. In addition to the scenes of feeding that she illustrated, she found that she could be symbolically nurtured through the process of Sandplay.

CONCLUSION

This chapter has provided what I hope is a useful overview of some of the issues that are amenable to Sandplay therapy. This is certainly not a complete summary of these types of cases, but its purpose is to give the reader an opportunity to compare his or her work with that of the author and to realize that no single avenue leads to the solution in any specific case. The examples chosen are ones that I have encountered. Other therapists may have different types of cases with different examples. That is what makes Sandplay unique: no two cases are ever exactly alike.

❦ 6 ❧

Examples of
Family Sandplay Therapy

This chapter illustrates two types of family sandplay therapy. The first case history shows how family sandplay was integrated with a child-centered sandplay process. I have designated this approach Child-Centered Family Sandplay. The second is a case that makes use of a family systems approach.

There are many situations where it is helpful and effective to include family members in the therapy of an individual child. This is often the case when a child begins to make some positive changes that temporarily unbalance family homeostasis. Additional times when it might be helpful to include other family members are when a child has a major intrafamily conflict with a sibling or a parent, when there has been a significant loss that affects all the family members, when a parent or sibling is in recovery from alcohol or drug addiction, or when a significant family member is incarcerated or terminally ill. Major family crises such as death, serious illness, a suicide threat, or acting out that affects each family member are other examples of situations when one might consider treating the family rather than one child.

The decision on when and how to include family members in a child's treatment is dependent on the particulars of each situation. Sometimes the entire family is treated at each session and the family, rather than one specified family member, becomes the therapy patient. At other times, treatment is begun with the individual child and the family is integrated into the treatment later. There are no rules to follow other than each therapist's clinical judgment. Often, some of the symptoms that are treated in child-centered cases can be just as effectively addressed through family intervention as through individual child therapy. The point where a therapist's clinical judgment is most important is during the assessment of the presenting situation, and can differ from one therapist to another. Two therapists might see two different interventions for the same case. The decision lies in the family dynamics and the assessment by each individual practitioner. There are no hard and fast rules as to which approach is the best; the best approach is the one that the therapist feels comfortable working with.

If a family crisis is involved, the major therapeutic decision confronting the therapist is most urgent: treatment of the entire family or of the individual child. This is one of those instances where there really is no right or wrong decision. A child is just one member of a family that has its own strengths and weaknesses and its own way of handling crises. He spends only one or two hours of each week with the therapist; the remainder of the time is spent with family, school, and peers. Inclusion of family members, whether used with a child-centered approach or a family systems approach, is beneficial not only to the child but to the family as well.

CHILD-CENTERED FAMILY SANDPLAY EXAMPLE

The case to be discussed here is that of an only child, age 4, who was living with both parents at the time I was asked to treat her. I shall call the child Evelyn.

The reason for this referral was that one afternoon Evelyn had drawn a picture in chalk on the driveway that she described as "a man with his peepee out who was standing next to a baby." She was also experiencing severe nightmares and night terrors. The day following this drawing, Evelyn told her nursery school teacher that her father had made her touch his penis. Her teacher asked her why, and her response was "because he likes me to do it." She went on to say that he did this when Mommy was not at home and that sometimes he even pulled down his pants. "Daddy likes me to hold my head way back, it makes him happy." Evelyn also reported that Daddy often slept with her. After this revelation, her teacher called in the nursery school principal and the child repeated the same story to her.

The principal called the mother, who immediately came to the school. The teacher and the principal reported to the mother what Evelyn had told them. Visibly distraught, the mother returned home and called her therapist, who referred Evelyn to me. I met with the child and her mother and then called the school. I was advised that Evelyn's behavior had become more and more difficult over the past year. She attacked other children for no apparent reason and attempted to hold boys' penises in the bathroom. The week before the reported incident she had asked one of the boys to urinate in the back yard of the school.

These facts were reported by the school to the Division for Youth and Family Services. Evelyn's father was arrested and put in jail, where he spent one night. The next morning he was released on his own recognizance. Evelyn's mother refused to allow him to return home, so he went instead to his mother's house. The father was advised that he could not have visitation privileges until such time as he was in therapy, and that the visits with Evelyn might be supervised. When I terminated with the child some three years later, the father still had not entered treatment and the child had not seen him or any of the other members of his family during that time. Evelyn's paternal grandmother was reported to have been her favorite grandma, which added to the child's feelings of loss and confusion. Her father's entire family fully supported him and insisted that the child had made up the story. At one point, shortly after the incident and before contact had been discontinued, Evelyn told her paternal grandmother that Daddy "made my peepee hurt." The grandmother told the child that she shouldn't say such things or Daddy and Mommy would be killed and go to heaven. I found this, and the behavior of many of the adults in her family, to be unconscionable—and yet it is fairly common in these types of cases.

The child's mother provided her own history as a means to help me treat Evelyn. She, herself, was an incest victim at age 4. Frequently, when a child has been molested, one finds that the parent had been abused at the same age as the child. The mother's incest was not perpetrated by her father, however, but by a friend of the family. She discovered this during flashbacks in her own therapy. During the time of Evelyn's suspected abuse her mother was out many evenings during the week. She told me that both she and her husband were drug and alcohol abusers. Mother was eating-disordered as well, and weighed between 300 and 350 pounds.

A mother's role is critical in understanding and treating the child victim. Adele Mayer (1983) describes the mother as the "silent partner" and lists characteristics common to these women (p. 30).

1. Poor self-image
2. Feelings of inadequacy as wife and mother
3. Strong dependency needs
4. Inability to take responsibility and cope with everyday problems
5. Passivity
6. Emotional immaturity, with infantile behavior
7. Sexual dysfunction
8. Denial as a defense mechanism
9. Guilt

Many of these characteristics were observed in Evelyn's mother.

After Evelyn revealed her story to her teacher, her mother began to make significant changes in her own life. She had already ceased her use of drugs and alcohol through her individual therapy. After Evelyn's revelation, she attended groups for incest survivors as well. She found community resources to support herself and the child, enrolled in college, instituted divorce proceedings, and generally handled the situation as well as she could. However, she was often in a dissociated state and was diagnosed as having a Dissociative Identity Disorder (*DSM-IV* 1994) during the time that I treated Evelyn.

A court trial was eventually held. The father made a plea bargain, which meant that Evelyn did not have to go to court to testify. He was put on probation for five years and ordered to pay all of the child's current therapy bills, as well as any future ones.

There were other symptoms Evelyn presented that were addressed during treatment and were directly related to the incest. For example, Evelyn would not use a public bathroom unless her mother accompanied her into the stall. This had led to some episodes of soiling her pants. This behavior was related to the fact that some of the episodes with her father had taken place in the bathroom. Her adjustment to public school was problematic because of the difficulty she experienced when she left the safety of her nursery school and was faced with an entirely new environment. She was unable to sit still, especially during story time. Instead, she wandered around the room, was disruptive, and refused to be drawn into any discussion. She was referred for psychological testing and was diagnosed as having Attention Deficit Hyperactivity Disorder and medicated with Ritalin.

Something that troubled Evelyn's mother was that Evelyn showed no reaction when she was hurt, denying that she experienced any pain at all. This is typical of traumatized children, because they learn to dissociate.

Individual Sandplay pictures made by Evelyn, some alone and some with her mother, follow.

Evelyn's first picture (Figure 6–1) contained ducks, a family of penguins, rhinoceroses, and hippopotamuses. Many of the figures are half-buried in the sand, which is something that I have observed in numerous cases of sexual abuse. It appears as if the patient cannot deal with the wound and the shame that accompanies it and so attempts to hide the injured part from view.

Figure 6–1

In noting the symbolism of the objects Evelyn chose, we observe that penguins live in a very cold climate, perhaps alluding to the lack of protection that she experienced from her environment. The hippopotamus, because of its voracious appetite, was designated in ancient Egypt to be an embodiment of evil powers as well as a symbol of brutality and injustice (Cirlot 1962). This choice of animal covers many levels in Evelyn's situation because it could refer to her mother's eating disorder as well as to her father's brutality. The ducks, according to Cirlot, were considered to be sacrificial animals, certainly an apt symbol for Evelyn.

The next Sandplay scene occurred about six months later. The therapeutic work during the intervening months was focused on helping Evelyn resolve the initial trauma and addressing her acting out against young males. The problem of her attempts to molest the boys at school was resolved fairly quickly. However, an infant male cousin became her next focal point. Several times she was stopped as she attempted to remove his diaper. Anatomical dolls were very useful during this period of therapy because she used the dolls as a way to express her aggression towards males.

Figures 6–2 and 6–3 were produced in the same session. Figure 6–2 shows castles under attack by dragons, with cavemen, rhinoceroses, and bunnies also present. The interpretation of the rhinoceros is the same as that of the hippopotamus in the earlier scene. The castle represents a fortress, a place of security for her, which was being attacked by dragons, many of them two-headed. The dragon, as we know from

Figure 6–2

Figure 6–3

many myths and fairy tales, is something to be overcome, an overpowering image. According to Jung (1956), the battle with dragons represents the battle between the ego and the regressive powers of the unconscious. The bunnies in this picture might represent, like the ducks in the first picture, her helpless, vulnerable side. Rabbits are also associated with sexuality because of their reproductive powers. One can readily see that the symbols chosen represent the situation of this patient.

In Figure 6–3, Evelyn portrayed a town with a rhinoceros on the roof of a house and several others roaming through the streets. Of note, however, is the empty center, which revealed exactly how she felt. She was not yet ready to face the interior void.

Evelyn went through a period of severe negative transference about a month prior to the production of these scenes. The acting out at nursery school had improved and she was now able to bring her rage into the open in the treatment setting. This indicated to me that she had developed sufficient trust in the therapeutic relationship to risk testing her rage. Her fury lasted about four to six weeks in extreme intensity. Because of the rage she was experiencing, Evelyn began to refuse to come into sessions at all, choosing instead to sit in the waiting room with her arms crossed. She openly defied me to make her come in. I interpreted this behavior as an expression of the deep rage she felt towards her father and mother. She now felt safe enough to project that rage onto me, something she eventually came to understand.

At this very explosive point I began to include Evelyn's mother in some of the sessions as a way to entice her to return to the playroom and because she had been expressing extreme separation anxiety from her mother. Evelyn's aggressive behavior towards me continued. She tried to kick me, to spit at me, and to express hatred verbally. I continued to interpret to her that I understood and accepted her rage, although I would not allow her to physically assault me. I explained that I knew her anger was related to the experience she had endured and reaffirmed that I cared for her, no matter how angry she might be.

In her next sand picture Evelyn set up the scene on the lid of the sandbox, rather than in the sand. There was a house with Superman and Batman asleep in a bed. A baby was beside Superman. Another baby slept in a crib. Superman and Batman, being superhuman, most likely referred to her father and perhaps also to her mother. The vulnerable baby was herself. At the end of the scene she added a hospital bed, which often is symbolic of the healing space of therapy.

When a child makes a scene on top of the sandbox, which occasionally happens, it could mean that the use of sand feels too threatening at that moment. I respect the child's right to choose this mode, if that is what is needed. Evelyn's negative transference was being resolved with this scene, and her acting out towards me began to abate.

Evelyn and her mother made the next scene (Figure 6–4), with Evelyn very much the director. They worked together to clear the center with a brush, then added many animals around the edge of the sand box. All of the animals, at this point, were domestic. This revealed that she had now moved to a more domesticated psychological level. The choice of animal in

Figure 6–4

Sandplay demonstrates the level of conflict in the psyche, with a dinosaur being a much more primitive level than a horse, for example. During the play that Evelyn enacted in response to this scene, different species of animals kissed each other: a dog kissed a cat; a horse kissed a cow. I felt this could have been her expression of the inappropriateness of sexual behavior between parent and child. The horse is a complex symbol that embodies both light and dark aspects, and it can often represent libidinal energies (Cirlot 1962).

I believe Figure 6–5 represented what was really in the center of the earlier pictures. These unseen feelings could not be exposed at the earlier times and Evelyn chose instead to leave the centers vacant. She used many snakes and dragons, and described the scene as "yucky." The trees in this scene

Figure 6–5

were added by Mother and symbolized her hope that growth would occur.

Figure 6–6 is a hospital scene representing a positive transference situation, with therapy viewed as a place of healing. In the play portion of this session, Evelyn fed her mother, me, and herself. She also made medicine for someone who she said was "bleeding to death in the waiting room," which represented how she must have felt on those occasions when she refused to leave the waiting room area. After she made the medicine, she went out to the waiting room and pretended to feed some people she said were there. The Hulk, another huge force, is visible in the picture but he is lying down, and a cave man is half buried. Evelyn was now beginning to get a sense of her own power and control. She once again illustrated the incest theme, with the figure of the half-buried cave man, but she had

Figure 6–6

tamed him, as well as Hulk, by having them beaten and lying down.

In the same session, Evelyn and Mom made Figure 6–7, which was reminiscent of several others that had animals and houses around the edge of the box. This time, however, Evelyn used shells to line the edges. Shells are a feminine symbol because they come from the sea. The Aphrodite myth tells us that she was borne to shore on a shell. In the center she made a river, with knights going across the bridges. This showed a tremendous amount of inner movement. She now had her inner protectors, the knights, in place, the river was flowing through the scene, and her femininity was emerging.

Figure 6–8 is another one Evelyn made with her mother. Evelyn buried all the marbles in my collection in this hill. Ini-

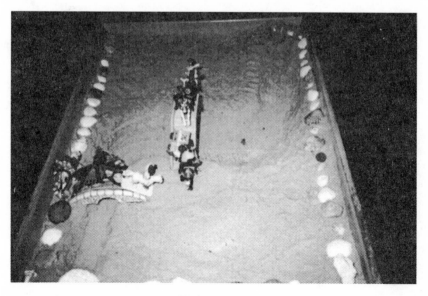

Figure 6–7

tially, all the figures were standing up. Then, very carefully (and at her direction), she and her mother laid them all down. She spent a great deal of time arranging the sand and patting it into the form that is seen in the picture. The hill and the sea (both indicative of the feminine) might suggest here that both Evelyn and her mother are resolving some of their feminine issues. I say this based on my observation of the tenderness with which this scene was produced. The marbles represented Evelyn's own inner treasure, which she has secured by burying them. The horses, lying down, are perhaps keeping her libidinal energy contained until she reaches the more appropriate developmental stage of adolescence.

The next several months we continued in this way, sometimes with Mother, sometimes with the child alone. Part of

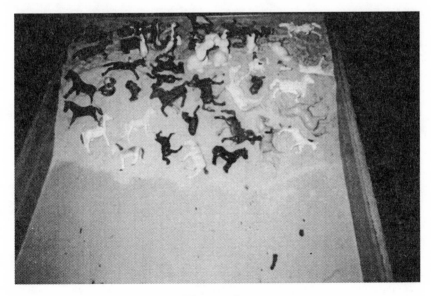

Figure 6–8

the work dealt with the possibility of a court appearance, which had renewed Evelyn's anxiety and caused some additional acting out. (Her appearance in court, however, was not necessary.)

The next picture (Figure 6–9) was made about six months after the previous one and was produced about three months after Evelyn had requested the resumption of individual treatment. By this time the separation issues with Mother had improved and there appeared to be no further threat of a court appearance. Evelyn used Smurfs, placing them in tepees. Some of the Smurfs were half buried. The small ones in the basket were also half buried in the sand. The half-buried figures reveal continued work on the incest theme. Cars (not visible) had been placed off to one side, out of the box. They were filled

Figure 6–9

and refilled with gasoline from a gas station. This type of scene, showing mechanized energy and the necessary gasoline to make the cars run, represented Evelyn being filled with new energy.

Figure 6–10 was produced on Evelyn's first day of kindergarten. On one side she set up a garden around a castle. On the other side she created a hospital scene with many patients. One patient was hidden behind a screen. Evelyn said that the patient's "peepee hurt" and only the doctor could see it. I asked her how it got hurt and she said the father did it. When I asked how he had hurt it, she changed the story and said the baby did it. This is an example of revealing trauma, then denying it and blaming oneself. Later, Evelyn moved to the other sand box and prepared food for everyone in the hospital. In this way she was able to soothe herself with the feeding scene. A baby

Figure 6–10

bottle is always visible in the play room and available to any child who might want it. Near the end of this session, Evelyn asked for it. I filled it and gave it to her. After revealing the trauma once again, she needed to regress to that early oral stage.

Evelyn began to rebel against kindergarten as a reaction to a renewed possibility that she might be called into court. This threat caused her to feel quite unsafe once again and she asked that her mother be included in the session that day. They did another combined picture (Figures 6–11 and 6–12). Each used half of the sandbox, which indicated to me that now boundaries were being observed. This is a rather remarkable picture. The overall shape is both phallic and breast-like. Evelyn's part, in the upper right corner, resembles the breast. She positioned the ladybug on top, where it kept slipping off.

Figure 6–11

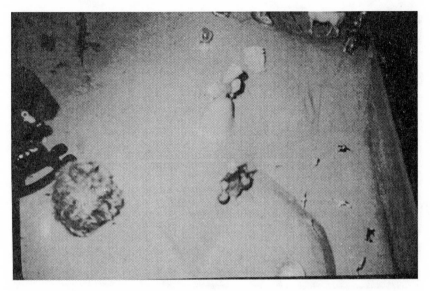

Figure 6–12

It appeared to me as if she were trying to put a nipple on the breast.

Her mother's area (foreground) revealed a very large phallic image. On it, Mom placed a wizard, a cobra, an hourglass, a good witch, a farm girl, a ball, baby Jesus, and a snake goddess. In the upper right corner of the box she made a special area she said was for a talking horse. In the lower right, she placed ice skaters. This seemed to reveal her mother's issues—a good wizard and good witch could make everything all right. There was also some fantasy material in the area of the talking horse, which indicated her very childlike qualities. The snake goddess most likely represented an aspect of her own sexual abuse, as well as that of Evelyn.

In looking at Evelyn's segment of this scene (Figure 6–13), one sees that she has constructed a castle and placed a temple on top of the castle, plus a ladybug, a telephone, and a ball.

Figure 6–13

In the blue water area are several houses, some horses, a large squirrel, a hedgehog, and a baby eating a pizza. Evelyn placed a boat in the canal between the two sections. Both Evelyn and her mother had difficulty telling any kind of story about their scenes, which may have been because of the underlying power of what they were witnessing. It was almost as if they were both awestruck by what was revealed, or it may have been that they could not yet find the words to describe what they were feeling.

After about two years of treatment, just prior to a session, I received a phone call from Evelyn's mother to report that she (Mother) had "lost it" that morning. Evelyn had allowed the dog to go out on a busy street after the dog had scratched her hand. She told her mother that she wanted to kill the dog. Her mother must have dissociated at that time and said to her, "Why don't you?" Evelyn said that she didn't have a gun.

Her mother grabbed a kitchen knife and said, "You don't need a gun. Here, I'll show you how to do it." At that point, Mother realized what she had done, but she and the child were both terrified. Later that morning she apologized to Evelyn and told her that this was inappropriate behavior. Evelyn, in an apparent attempt to ease Mother's guilt, told her several things about "what my brain says to me," the gist of it being that she missed Daddy and that her brain sees that she and Mommy are bad. This was a painful illustration of the dynamics between these two victims. During the session that afternoon, Evelyn, her mother, and I discussed all the out-of-control feelings that had occurred that morning and how the process of dissociating can cause serious repercussions. Both felt relieved after the session.

Several weeks later Mother came into a session and said that Evelyn had a lot to discuss because Mom had gone on her first date the previous night. The date was not successful, according to Mother, but Evelyn had the fantasy that her mother had married again and had had another baby. The fantasy was twofold. First was Evelyn's fear that she might lose her place as the only child. Second was the hope that she might one day have a normal family. The scene that she made that day was a Christmas one with many houses, Santa in the center with a Christmas tree, his sleigh full of toys, and a reindeer. This seemed to illustrate Evelyn's hope (and Mother's) that there was a happy future in store for them.

Figure 6–14 is an elaborate scene with people, animals, and bridges. This illustrates Evelyn's growth and the fact that she had available energy for further growth, indicated by the inclusion of gasoline stations. (As noted previously, gasoline provides energy for mechanized vehicles.) One unsettling aspect of the picture is the baby in the crib with no one to care for it.

Figure 6–14

This might have been another instance of a previous feeling that she was unprotected by the adults in her family. It might also represent the fantasy of her mother giving birth to another child and her unconscious wish to exclude it. Upon completion of this picture, Evelyn took all the snakes and insects from the shelf and threw them into the other box. She did not want to touch them, but she did feed a big cobra and a crocodile. She was showing me that in one box there was growth, but in the other more dangerous material remained.

Evelyn's next scene (Figure 6–15) was that of two sisters. Part of it she described as being outdoors, the other indoors. Each sister had her own special horse from the herd, which was outside. She said the sisters owned many horses. (Some of the horses Evelyn used are made with small pegs on top of them and the human figures have holes underneath so that the figures can be secured on top of the horses.) The inside part of the scene showed the sisters' bedrooms, accessible by a set of steps. At one point, Evelyn removed the larger figures that are made to go astride some of the horses and replaced them with smaller figures. I made an interpretation that referred to the genital suggestiveness of the pegs and holes in these figures. (Other children had laughingly pointed this out to me when they had taken the figures from the shelf to play with.) I told Evelyn that holes in the miniature human figures were for the purpose of securing the rider to the horse. I said that girls, too, have holes inside of them that are called vaginas, and that they could hurt if inappropriate things were placed in them, such as an adult penis. I was quite graphic with her, in the hope that this would provide further integration and resolution of her

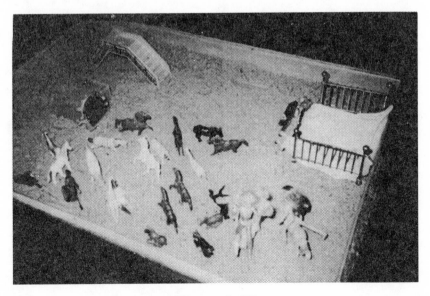

Figure 6–15

trauma. This appeared to be the case, because Evelyn made no comment and went to the other sand box where she began to make a cake, which she then fed to her mother and me. This symbolic feeding was her way to let me know that she understood what I had tried to convey, and to illustrate the nurturance that she was receiving. It might also have been a distraction for her—using food to soothe and to avoid facing trauma.

The incest issue had been addressed throughout Evelyn's therapy in various ways. Sandplay, art work, and anatomical dolls were the major tools and techniques utilized. However, her use of the horse and rider figures at this terminal phase of treatment presented an additional opportunity to graphically illustrate the incest issue for her. This was the last of the sand pictures that Evelyn made over a period of three years.

My work with Evelyn and, when requested, with her mother, continued for some months longer in order to allow stabilization to occur. It is likely, however, that Evelyn will again require treatment when she approaches adolescence. At the conclusion of sandplay treatment, she and her mother were rebuilding a comfortable life together. Mother completed her education and resumed full-time employment. Her mothering skills were vastly improved and she continued to pursue her own recovery issues.

FAMILY SANDPLAY THERAPY

The second example to be presented in this chapter is a family that was in crisis when they entered therapy. When a case is of crisis proportions one can assume that all members of the family are suffering, so a family systems model is often the most efficient way to treat the family members.

I will call this family the D.s. There were three children in the family whom I shall call Naomi (age 15), Anthony (age 11), and Michael (age 9½). Naomi was not present for the intake session, as she was the cause of the family crisis. She had been hospitalized after ingesting a very large quantity of liquor. She was taken from the emergency room of the local hospital directly to an inpatient unit that specialized in teenage drug and alcohol problems. The situation was diagnosed as a suicide attempt. Psychological testing was administered while she was hospitalized and she was diagnosed with Conduct Disorder and Oppositional Disorder (*DSM-IV* 1994). The parents also learned that she had been inducing vomiting for several months.

The D.s told me that Naomi had always been an oppositional child and was quite difficult to handle. Her maladaptive behavior dated back as far as preschool. She had been taken to other therapists, none of whom she could relate to. In the eighth grade, after being diagnosed with Attention Deficit Disorder with Hyperactivity, she was enrolled in a school for learning disabled children and medicated with Dexedrine. She was mainstreamed into a regular classroom for the ninth grade and her school work continued to be poor. She barely passed the ninth grade and was in tenth grade when I started to treat the family.

The D.s' second child, Anthony, age 11, was in the fifth grade. He too presented with problems. He was described as "unbearable" by his parents and had problems with friends and teachers. He wanted to be "the best" at everything he attempted, and had serious mood swings when things did not turn out the way he wanted. Anthony was scheduled for extra help at school for comprehension problems, but often did not attend because he "didn't like it."

The third child, Michael, age 9½, was diagnosed with Attention Deficit Hyperactive Disorder, and had been medicated with Ritalin for the past two years. He was in a self-contained classroom for children with similar problems. Both boys had been very upset over Naomi's hospitalization.

None of the children got along with each other. Father was reported to be the disciplinarian, his method being to send them to their rooms. Mom's comment on his form of discipline was, "Yes, they are sent to their rooms and then they trash them." The foregoing information was obtained during the intake session with the parents.

At the time of the first family session, Naomi was still in the hospital and the parents had no idea how long she might be there. The boys accompanied their parents to this session but were quite restless. In order to lessen the tension level, I suggested that perhaps everyone could draw a picture of the family. They were quite agreeable to this suggestion, except for Michael, who clung to his mother and refused to draw. At the last moment he added the family cat to Mom's drawing. After they had all completed their pictures, I said that they could share the pictures with one another.

Anthony became enraged at this suggestion and furiously erased part of his drawing (Figure 6–16). Earlier in the session he had asked if we could all go into the sandplay room, and was told that we would not do that until after the pictures had been shared. He said that was bribery, but he did cooperate. His picture is difficult to decipher because of the erasures, but one can sense the frenzy and anxiety that pervade it.

Figure 6–17 was made by Mom. It is interesting to see how she has placed the figures. Each is separated from the other, and each is involved with his or her own interests. Anthony is

Figure 6–16

rollerblading, Michael is playing tennis, Naomi is listening to music, and Dad is building something. Mom is at the bottom of the page, as if she were carrying the whole load while going off to work.

Dad's picture (Figure 6–18) is somewhat unusual. They all have identical grins on their faces. None of the figures has hands, feet, or clothes, and all are suspended above ground. I commented about how the family members all had to keep smiles on their faces, no matter how serious things were. I was alluding to the fact that one of their members was in the hospital. My unspoken interpretation of this picture was that no one in the family was grounded (because of the placement of

Figure 6–17

the figures above the ground line), all were angry and impotent (no hands), and all were unsure of how to present themselves to others (inappropriate grins) and felt totally exposed (no clothes).

The boys were anxious to go to the sandplay room, so the desired sharing of the pictures did not occur. Since this was the first full family session, I was assessing the overall situation to determine the most effective method to treat this family. We went to the other room, where Anthony worked frenetically in the sand, tossing it to and fro. It seemed as if he could not do enough. He changed his sandplay scene at least three times before producing this one of Indians and a burial ground (Figure 6–19). There are many figures on the edge of the sand box, indicating that Anthony is not yet sure whether to enter fully into the process. The burial ground might have both indicated his wish to bury the fact of his sister's hospitalization and illustrated the anxiety and rage this engendered in him. Anthony followed this with another scene (Figure 6–20), an army communication center with an ambulance in the upper left corner. I felt that he was trying to make certain I had received the message (in his first scene) of anxiety, shame, and anger, and that he saw the possibility for family healing in the ambulance.

Michael made a war scene with a lake in the center and a diver in the lake (Figure 6–21). Because these were the boys' first sand constructions, I withheld verbal comments. Both

Figure 6–18

Figure 6–19

Figure 6–20

Figure 6–21

of Anthony's scenes were warlike and graphically portrayed his struggle. The second of his scenes included attempts at communication, which were what this family desperately needed. Michael's scene was also warlike, but he included a large water area with underwater divers, which might be viewed as a positive signal that he was ready to dive into the unconscious.

My impression after this second session (the first with the two sons) was that Anthony was the family spokesperson as far as enacting the underlying dynamics. He demonstrated the anger and frenzy that were felt by all. When the session was ending he did not want to leave and asked what we could do next. With only a few minutes left, I offered them nonhardening clay. This is good for monster making and smashing, which allows for release of anger. Both boys made monsters and seemed to enjoy smashing them. (I have a large hammer called a "Schmusser" for this purpose that I had shown them.)

Naomi remained in the hospital for almost seven weeks. Family sessions continued, and could best be described as volatile, with the focus of attention alternating between Anthony and Michael.

During one session Anthony became extremely angry and ran out of the office. Dad brought him back and we all gathered in the sand room. He said that he only wanted to go home. He expressed hatred towards me, adding that he would kill me by bringing a knife from home next time. I responded by saying that I knew he was very angry, but that I believed it was related to the confusion in his family and the fact that the family was coming here because of all the fears related to Naomi's hospitalization.

At another point during the session, Anthony referred to the fact that his sister was in a "mental hospital." I attempted to explore his feelings about that, but he refused to answer. I believe that he identified me with all of his problems. When this dynamic was interpreted to him, he vehemently denied it. Quite often in this type of volatile situation a family member will externalize the problem until the time when he is able to accept these interpretations.

Michael occupied himself by constructing a sand picture containing a Chinese junk on a hill, a skier going down one side of the hill, cars and houses on another side, a lake with a boat on it, and many marbles (which Michael said were treasure). The Hulk stood looking at the scene. Near the end of the session, just as I was about to photograph Michael's picture, Anthony stomped over to the box and wiped out all of Michael's work with one aggressive swoop of his arm, causing Michael to scream and cry. Anthony then violently manipulated the sand, over and over. He seemed to be trying to calm himself in this way. As the family was leaving, I asked Mrs. D. to call me the following day because I had serious concerns about Anthony. I planned to discuss a referral for a psychiatric evaluation for him, as I felt that he too might need medication. Mrs. D. agreed to the psychiatric referral and we scheduled an appointment. Unfortunately, the evaluation had to be postponed for several weeks due to the psychiatrist's tight schedule.

After the seventh week of family therapy, I met Naomi for the first time. The original plan had been to have a session with Naomi and both parents, before including the boys. However, no babysitter was available, so Dad stayed home with the boys and the session was held with only Mom and Naomi. I found Naomi somewhat subdued, allowing Mom to do most of the reporting. She did contribute, however, that she was not suicidal and never had been. She said she had been merely "experimenting" with alcohol.

The next session, again with only Mom and Naomi, found Naomi "out for bear," belligerent and uncooperative. Her affect was very much like Anthony's. Throughout the session she seemed to be quite lethargic as well as angry and defensive. The lethargy probably stemmed from the medication she was now taking.

She became enraged at her mother during this session, because Mom had thrown out some posters and records of hers while she was in the hospital. Some of these contained material glorifying death, and Mother insisted she did not want "those things" in her house. However, Naomi pointed out that it was her mother who had bought them for her. Mother had a forced smile through the entire session, but really appeared worn out. The forced smile was reminiscent of Dad's drawing in our first session.

The tenth session was the first one attended by all five family members. During the early part of the session Mom related all that had transpired in order to gain Naomi's readmission to school, which was quite an undertaking. Both parents were enraged at the school for the roadblocks they felt had been put in the way. Naomi was refused entrance to the recommended post-hospital program because of her oppositional stance, so had to return to her regular high school. The session began in my formal office where I tried to explore with Naomi how her adjustment to school had been. She responded in a defensive, angry way. The boys became restless and wanted to go into the playroom, rather than just talk.

We did go into the playroom, where Anthony drew a portrait of Mom. It showed clearly how he saw her: quite angry and with teeth bared. Then he drew a picture of Dad with a silly, inane grin on his face. As Anthony drew, Michael and Mom set up a war scene in the sand with soldiers, flags, and parasols (Figure 6–22). Naomi observed them, then began to construct her own scene. Dad found the hospital miniatures and put them into the scene Naomi was setting up. I had expected her to object, but she did not. Dad said that he chose the hospital toys because he is a male nurse in the reserves.

After Anthony finished his drawing he moved to the wet sand box and made another scene. He formed a mound in the sand, then placed another mound on top of that, with a hole in the center. He added Mexican figures to the scene, a flag on top of the mound, and two madonnas guarding the gate. There was a Chinese temple in a phallic shape, positioned as

Figure 6–22

if aimed at him. It was a very complex picture. Anthony asked that I not photograph this one. He talked about how he wanted to be an explorer and find a place like this, or else to be a builder and build one.

The boys then decided they wanted to use clay, and they involved Naomi in that activity with them. She and Anthony revealed some artistic ability in their creative use of the clay. Anthony made a monster that was similar to his drawings, with its open mouth and evident oral rage. Naomi's was the complete figure of a girl. Michael became somewhat agitated because his piece did not go the way he had envisioned. I put a calming hand on him; his parents seemed immobilized.

Some weeks later, a parent conference session was held with Mrs. D. It had been scheduled for both parents, but

Mr. D. was unable to attend because of a work emergency. Mrs. D. reported that everyone in the house did nothing but scream at one another. A first request to the children to do something never worked, so with each subsequent request the screaming escalated. She was concerned that Naomi seemed to be sleeping most of the time, which she attributed to the medication. Naomi had become obstinate and nonproductive in her individual therapy (which had been arranged by the hospital), and Mrs. D. was not sure how much longer she could force her to go. Mom reported that Michael was "just Michael." He never admitted to doing anything wrong. Anthony continued to have problems in school with the teachers and his peers. She said that she received a telephone call every single day from school about at least one of the children, sometimes about two or all three. She felt completely overwhelmed. Mrs. D. thought that Mr. D. might also have Attention Deficit Hyperactivity Disorder, explaining that he never sat but always stood or paced. She told me that he had a hard time getting through school, but managed to graduate from college through sheer determination.

Mom and the three children came to a subsequent session without Dad who, once again, was unable to attend because of an emergency call. Anthony had seen the psychiatrist twice for the evaluation, but the second test had not been completed so he would have to go back again in two weeks. Mom reported that Anthony did not feel well physically or emotionally on the day of the second evaluation. He had performed poorly in a track meet earlier that afternoon, and this had upset him so much that he could not be properly evaluated by the psychiatrist. (I suggested perhaps she should take his temperature when they went home, which she did and found that he was running a slight fever. She telephoned me with this information the next day.)

Michael and Naomi wanted to paint in this session. Michael's work ended in a fingerpaint mélange; Naomi painted a beautiful bowl of flowers in a black vase, with a gray shadow under it (which seemed to speak of her depression). Anthony then suggested that we go into the other room to talk, which we did. But he felt sick and did not participate much. The children reported that Mom and Dad had tried very hard to quit yelling, so the week had been quieter.

In another full family session two weeks later, Naomi was quite distraught about an incident that had occurred at home. Michael had found cigarettes in Naomi's purse and had told Anthony, who then told Mom. Naomi denied they were hers. Mom said that she wanted the truth, since this was the third time Naomi had been caught with cigarettes. In the session, major conflict erupted between Dad and Naomi over the incident, which sent Anthony into hysterics. He banged his head, kicked his feet, and was totally overwrought. Michael's behavior was bizarre. He made weird faces as he tried to mimic the others.

There was a strained beginning to another family session that was held without Michael, who had been invited to go away with a friend. In the early part of the session Naomi refused to participate, which provoked Anthony. There had been an incident between Naomi and Mom earlier in the week, when Naomi was exceedingly abusive towards Mom. This had infuriated Anthony, because he felt the problem could have easily been resolved. Naomi had apologized to Mom the next day, but despite this she was grounded for a week. Anthony thought that Mom had forgiven her too easily, so that the punishment was ineffective. We discussed Anthony's tendency to take on a parental role.

Naomi attempted to change the subject and initiated a discussion about a motorcycle. Dad had one, and Naomi wanted to learn to ride it. Anthony became furious, saying that she would wreck it and then he could not have it when he turned 16. Nothing could make him recognize the fact that he would not be 16 for several years, and that Naomi had just turned 16, the legal age to ride a motorcycle. The D.s said that, if she could prove that she was "responsible" (their term), she would be allowed to use it.

Then the family anger turned towards me. Anthony accused me of not doing anything but observing. He dared me to solve their problems. Dad also interjected that he was tired of coming here, which opinion was echoed by Naomi. I told Anthony that I thought there was a tremendous amount of destructive anger in this family that was keeping everyone upset, not just him and Naomi. He verbalized extreme hatred towards his sister for all the trouble she had caused and said that he wished she would really disappear. I told Anthony that I could not change the family's behavior in one hour a week and that all of them had to think of ways to make it better for themselves. We used some role reversal techniques during this session, but no one wanted to be the therapist.

Mrs. D. reported to me by telephone that Anthony's assessment with the psychiatrist had now been completed. He was not medicated at this time, as the psychiatrist felt that family therapy was the best modality for this child. I did not agree with this decision.

One session scheduled for the two boys alone turned out to be a fiasco. Each boy went to one sand box and set up his own war scene. They then proceeded to demolish each other's work. Michael said something that angered Anthony, who then began to punch him unmercifully. For a short while I was able to physically restrain Anthony, but he was too strong for me and I had to release him. Their father had dropped them off for the session and then left on some errands, so there was no parent present to be of assistance.

After a semblance of order was restored, I suggested that the boys could make a combined sandplay scene. They did cooperate and set up an Indian village, which was not photographed, at Anthony's request.

A verbal session, one without art or sand, was held in the formal office with the entire family. A serious conflict had arisen between Naomi and her parents about another incident at school. As a result of the incident, Naomi was to be suspended from school for two days. Her mother was incensed because Naomi had already missed so much school. After numerous phone calls, Mom succeeded in arranging for Naomi to be readmitted to school after only one day's suspension. In the family session Naomi appeared irrational, as she tried to defend herself. Dad tried unsuccessfully to "make her see reason." He became verbally abusive, and the battle escalated. Mom's role was that of the intermediary. I suggested that she allow Dad and Naomi to address their own relationship issues, but she continued to play family peacemaker throughout.

Anthony became enraged at one point in this session when I revealed how the boys had behaved when he and Michael were here alone. I used this as a way to help the family begin to address conflicts in more appropriate ways, without screaming or physical attacks on one another. I do not know whether this was successful. Anthony kept demanding that we move to the sand room, but there was so much being revealed verbally at that time that the session was concluded in the main office.

The sessions continued for several months with various combinations of family members and with formats that ranged from art to sand to verbalization. The expression of anger, without physical abuse, continued to be the focus of therapy.

The parents had purchased a new, larger home that they believed might improve the family relationships as they would not be so cramped. After some remodeling, they planned to move. This would entail a change of school for all the children, which would also offer them a new start. No one in the new district would know of Naomi's hospitalization, which everyone in the family had experienced as a difficult issue to face with friends and neighbors.

One week I had scheduled Naomi and Mom, but Naomi and Dad appeared instead. The reason given for the change was that Naomi and Mom were not speaking, but in the discussion that followed it became clear that it was Naomi who was not speaking to Mom. She had written a letter to a pen pal, had stamped it, and put it out for the postman. Mom had later made an allusion to something that Naomi had written in the letter, so Naomi knew that Mom had opened it and read it. This left her feeling totally violated and invaded. I did not know what Mom had read in the letter and it was not revealed in the discussion. Dad tried to defend Mom, while I tried to defend Naomi's right to privacy, which was not much respected in the family. My expressed concern was that Naomi should not be kept under a microscope, for this would lead to further acting out. During the heated argument at home, Mom had told Naomi that she needed to be put in a mental hospital. Dad was the go-between and the only one Naomi was willing to relate to, at least during this session.

At the time of the following session, Mom and Naomi were still not talking. That session was held with Mom and the boys. Mom reported that Naomi's psychiatrist had said that Mom had no business opening Naomi's letter. I commented that Mom must have felt attacked on all fronts, because I had said the same thing. She nodded, yes she did, but went on to explain that Naomi had sealed the letter in front of her, stamped it and double sealed it with Scotch tape, as if she really wanted Mom to notice. And Mom had complied. Anthony kept badgering Mom about what she found in Naomi's letter. She said that it was inappropriate to tell him, but I commented on how destructive family secrets can be, so she revealed it. (I was certain that eventually the information would have been disclosed by someone.) Naomi's letter revealed that she and a friend had observed a man masturbating in public and found this quite amusing. All of this was extremely disturbing to the mother. I urged Mom to tell Naomi that her brothers knew what was in the note because I was sure they would find a way to tell her themselves, and it would be better coming from Mom.

Only Mom and Naomi came to the next session. Naomi was an "accident waiting to happen" in her fury. She expressed extreme hatred towards me since she knew that Mom had revealed the contents of her letter to me, and hatred towards "this place." I attempted to show her that she was, in fact, feeling invaded by all adults, but primarily by her mother, because it was her mother who had opened her letter. Confrontation then ensued between Naomi and Mom over Mom's intrusiveness, rules, and regulations.

Later, Mom and Dad came for a parenting session to reassess the entire situation. I expressed my concern that Naomi might need to be rehospitalized for additional treatment. According to Dad, however, Naomi had been much better that week. Mom said that was true, because Naomi had gotten everything she wanted the past week. She went to *The Rocky Horror Picture Show*, was going to a gym, and had begun to take an art class at a local community college.

They told me that the child psychiatrist had met again with Anthony and that he now said Anthony was diagnosed with Attention Deficit Hyperactive Disorder in addition to being depressed. He recommended a medication that would address both problems, or Ritalin as an alternative. Mom had looked up both medications and decided they might give Ritalin a trial, since it had fewer side effects.

The family sessions continued for a number of weeks, but the intensity of anger seemed diminished. Anthony was told that he would need to have a neurological examination prior to taking the recommended medication. He was quite verbal with his parents in a session saying that he did not want to do this at all. We discussed the advantages and disadvantages of taking medication or not taking it, but Anthony kept insisting that he did not need it.

Anthony argued incessantly throughout the session, stating that he hated all adults except his family, hated school, and hated coming here. It was noted, however, that he appeared less volatile than on previous occasions. Mom said that she was considering the medication, but had not completely made up her mind. I suggested that if Anthony were to begin medication he should start before school began so that he would have a chance to adjust to it.

The next family session was held without Naomi. She had gone to a concert, but was to be grounded the following week as punishment for not attending family therapy with the rest of the family. Michael became restless, so we went into the playroom and began with clay. Anthony tried to jam up the press that is used to make hair. I asked him to please use less clay, so that would not happen. He got angry, threw the clay down, went to the sand box and started to make rainfalls of sand. After a brief time, I commented on his anger, which he tried to deny, but Mom supported my observation.

Each boy then began to make his own scene. Anthony did not want Dad to see his until it was finished. When completed (Figure 6–23), it contained two oil wells connected with a string, a deep sea diver, soldiers, and tanks. He was angry because he thought Michael had used all the soldiers, but I pointed out that there were smaller ones he could use and that they really fit into his picture better anyway. He seemed content with this, and his Dad gave him appropriate praise, so Anthony felt positive about the scene that he made.

Michael's scene (Figure 6–24) contained all the larger soldiers and a water area in the center, with boats poised for action. Near the end of the session, Dad added a cowboy on a horse to Michael's scene, which Michael did not notice until after I had taken the picture. When he saw it, he became furious at Dad and stormed out of the room. When he came back in, I tried to help him see that perhaps Dad just wanted to play with him.

There was a session attended only by Mom, Dad, and Anthony, although I had expected everyone. Mom reported that Naomi was not there because she had come home from school with the name and phone number of a therapist and

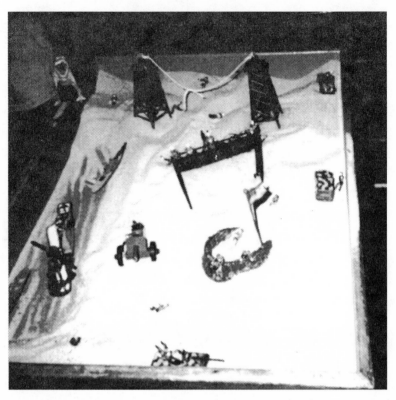

Figure 6–23

asked if she could see this therapist, who had been highly recommended by a friend of hers. Mom had agreed, and an appointment had been scheduled for the following day. Naomi
felt that because she would have her own therapist, she no
longer needed to come to family sessions. Her mother, fearing
Naomi's rage, had permitted the absence, which was addressed
in the session.

The family made a geographical move prior to the beginning of the next school term. This meant that each of the children would be in different buildings. Michael was in elemen-

tary school, Anthony in middle school, and Naomi in high school. Part of the family therapy during those weeks focused on changes that each child could anticipate in the new settings. It was discussed as the possibility of a new start for each of them.

Counseling and tutoring were provided for Michael in his school as part of his special education program. Anthony was seen by a community counselor, since he was new in that school. He was quite unhappy with his new teacher, whom he described as a "yeller." Anthony made some drawings through much of this session, and left behind a frightening picture. It was intended to be the figure of a rollerblader, but the face was

Figure 6–24

grisly. He titled it "Dead X End—Rollerblade." He was in better control in this session, because his siblings were not present.

Naomi refused to attend further family sessions, since she had begun to see the other therapist. I concurred with this decision because of her noncompliance in family therapy. The new therapist had told Mrs. D. that she would not see the parents at all, unless she felt that there was the possibility of danger of some kind.

This was a managed-care case and termination had been suggested by the family's plan. The sessions had begun to reveal slight improvement in the family situation and Mom reported that there had been a couple of weeks of relative quiet. We discussed the possibility of termination in the near future.

In a subsequent session, the boys expressed the wish to go into the sandplay room, which we did. They both wanted to pound the clay for a while, then each did a similar sand picture that depicted an army in some trees. Anthony's was the more aggressive picture. He and Dad rigged up a plane so that it would fly overhead. At the end of the session, Anthony got angry when I refused to allow him to use the camera to take the Polaroid picture. (It is one of my few rules that I operate both of the cameras.) He immediately began to disassemble his tray and put things away, so that I could not take a picture of it, and left the room. I said that I guessed he was angry at me once again and I was sorry that this was how he chose to handle his anger. In addition to the trees and soldiers in Michael's picture, he had some treasure strewn around and a beautiful red bird perched on top of a tree. I gave him a lot of credit and support for his creativity.

There was a holiday break, after which I expected to meet with the four family members, but only the parents arrived.

They reported that everything seemed to be much better, although Dad said that anger was still a paramount issue. Naomi continued to see the therapist she had chosen and seemed to be improving at home, although a terrible progress report in all of her subjects had been received from school. She was either turning in no homework or homework that was incomplete.

In another parent session with Mr. and Mrs. D. they reported that Naomi was pretty much the same, but that Mom was just "letting it be," at least as much as possible. Michael was Michael, and Anthony had shown much improvement. They said that Anthony was trying hard in his schoolwork and in socialization. I suggested that the next session be scheduled as a family one in order to plan for termination.

The family arrived without Naomi for the next session. Mom announced at the beginning of the session that the family had decided they would like this to be the last session, with the option left open to return if need be. I felt we had probably made as many gains as possible at that time, and so I agreed.

The reports at that session were that Naomi was in Las Vegas with a friend and the friend's family. The D.'s were expecting a 10-year-old French student shortly, after which Anthony was to spend a week or two in France. Michael was going to Cape Cod on a class trip and was angry because he was not allowed to go anywhere alone. The remainder of the session was a review of how far the family members had come since they began, and how well they had all adjusted to Naomi's hospitalization and to the move to a new house and new schools. Anthony still did not like the kids in the new school, but was trying to adjust. He seemed to have a more positive attitude. Michael was to be mainstreamed in several classes next year and would then attend the middle school. Naomi might attend a local community college, but this would depend on how well she completed the current school year.

CONCLUSION

The D. family was treated for a little over a year in a family therapy format. Many of the sessions were with the entire family with the exception of Naomi, who attended until she found her own therapist. The other sessions were held with different combinations of family members.

The major treatment focus began with Naomi's hospitalization and its effects on the entire family. The issues covered included the fear and anger engendered by each family member. Much of the therapeutic work was focused on an appropriate expression of anger and control. Each had his or her own authority issues, which became a stumbling block at some times.

Michael had serious learning disabilities, which will cause additional stress for him as he develops. However, he was in an appropriate setting to address his needs. Anthony had an extreme need for perfection, which might lead to undue stress as he approaches adolescence.

Mr. D. had perhaps been learning disabled himself although, through sheer will power, he had been able to graduate from college. Mrs. D. was also a college graduate and had professional employment. Mr. D. was the authority figure in the family and Mrs. D. supported him. Each child had a strong need to establish autonomy, which caused rebellion and upheaval within the family system.

Treatment was designed to address the needs of each family member in a way that would enable them to begin to change their communication patterns. The methods used were both verbal and nonverbal and included both sandplay therapy and art therapy, examples of which are included in this chapter. The D. family experienced problems of crisis proportions with the children, but ultimately achieved some measure of stabilization.

◖◗ 7 ◖◗

The Person of the Therapist

There are many professionals from various orientations who affirm that true healing in therapy is contingent upon the person of the therapist, how personally centered, professionally developed, and knowledgeable she is, and how well she can address the issues of transference and countertransference in therapy. It is just as important for the Sandplay therapist and the family systems practitioner to possess these qualities as it is for any other type of therapist.

The Sandplay therapist, as well as the therapist who chooses to treat families with the sandplay technique, needs to be well versed in several theoretical bases. Graduate education in psychology, psychiatry, social work, and/or counseling is essential. Some experience in the areas of play, family, and individual therapy is also desirable, especially for those who use sandplay with families. Training in Sandplay therapy itself is essential, whether it is practiced from a Jungian individual base or a family systems one. In addition, some understanding, training, and experience with art therapy, though not essential, is a definite advantage. (Conversely, the art therapist who uses Sandplay should have additional training in Sandplay.) I am firmly convinced that no one should undertake the practice of Sandplay in any form without specific training in the field and I believe the practitioner needs experience not only as a therapist but also as a client.

I have always been amazed by the large number of therapists who provide treatment to others and yet have never had any therapy for themselves. It is like trying to ride a horse while wearing blinders. The horse can proceed on its own path, but the rider cannot see the hidden dangers, such as low-hanging branches or other obstacles that are in the way. So it is with therapy—one can only take a patient as far as one has been able to go oneself. The blinders cannot be on. One needs clear vision and understanding in order to practice any form of therapy.

The art of Sandplay is no exception. I believe it is essential to have adequate personal experience with the medium before one undertakes its practice with clients. Adequate experience is hard to define and is dependent upon one's personality structure combined with one's personal history. A single trial experience doing a Sandplay construction is not sufficient training for a person to appreciate the depths that can be achieved with Sandplay therapy, nor is attendance at one or two workshops.

The first Sandplay experience for an adult, whether as a trainee or as a client, is usually a testing ground and is often undertaken with some timidity. One is faced with a broad assortment of miniatures and asked to make a picture. Adults have varied reactions to such a task. Sometimes the reaction is "I don't know what to do," or "This is just for kids." An attempt may be made to portray a scene from life or a dream, or the adult may become immobilized because the experience is unknown and frightening. Any of these reactions is possible when one first attempts to produce a sand picture. This provides a real learning experience to the novice Sandplay therapist about the power inherent in this medium. Strong visceral reactions are possible at any stage of a Sandplay process, which is why it is essential that one who chooses to use this technique be as fully experienced and as well trained as possible. Sometimes people ask, "How many sessions of Sandplay do I need in order to achieve a complete process?" There is no possible way to determine this, as one never knows what will be encountered during Sandplay therapy at the beginning of treatment. One can only deal with this issue on a session by session basis, just as one does with dream analysis or any other form of traditional therapy.

Individual Sandplay therapy offers an opportunity to touch the deepest archetypal layer of the psyche, which is the reason it can be so powerful and, at the same time, why it can be so threatening. The adult is often loath to expose that part of herself to another in this manner, feeling that she is being judged by an expert observer. It is only through experiencing all the feelings that go into the production of a Sandplay picture that the novice Sandplay therapist can truly understand the reactions of fear, humiliation, exhilaration, or awe that are often aroused in the patient.

There are some therapists who attempt to make a sand picture by themselves. This is not recommended, because one needs a witness to share the inherent power in this process.

The possibility of uncovering material at such a deep, symbolic level requires gentle care, protection, and nurturance. Dora Kalff always referred to the sand box as a "free and protected space." It needs to be kept protected.

If one chooses not to go to a trained Jungian Sandplay practitioner in order to experiment with the process, one might elect to share the experience with an interested colleague, although I do not recommend this unless the colleague has some familiarity with the technique. The "objective other" is, however, essential, no matter how one opts to experience Sandplay. One reason, as already pointed out, is the need for protection. Another is that we all have blinders on regarding our own psychic process. Interpreting one's own Sandplay picture is similar to interpreting one's own dreams, in that we tend to see only what is comfortable for us to see. It is quite easy to keep our shadow material in the dark.

I vividly recall the first Sandplay experience I ever had with Kalff, and the emotional connection that I encountered, both to Frau Kalff and to this unknown technique. I felt as if I had somehow been struck by an unknown something that I can only call "power." I had sought her out because, from the first lecture I heard her deliver, I was impressed by her warmth, patience, acceptance, poise, knowledge, and presentation of the material—all of the qualities identified with my belief that it is the person of the therapist that is the ultimate healing factor. I was privileged to experience many individual sessions under the caring eye of Frau Kalff. She has been a positive role model for me and many others who were fortunate enough to train with her.

Other important information that I believe is needed by a Jungian Sandplay therapist is a working knowledge of Jung's theories of psychological types (Jung 1976) which was touched on in Chapter One. Some familiarity with the Myers-Briggs Inventory (1962) is useful in understanding how this theory can apply to Sandplay. It is quite helpful for therapists to know their own typology as well as that of their patients, so there can be an awareness of how the types interact. When one has some knowledge of personality types, it is possible to deepen and enhance the interpretation of a sand picture.

For example, I have taken the Myers-Briggs, and the scoring found me to be an INFP (Introverted, with Feeling and Intuition as my strong functions). This means that my Thinking and Sensation functions are not as well developed as the others. Applying this knowledge to my practice as a Sandplay therapist has enabled me to strengthen my weaker functions. I have found it less difficult to strengthen my Thinking function than my Sensation function because abstract thinking is required for professional training to attain a diploma (and to write a book). Sensation has always given me the most trouble. It is the quality that enables us to read a map, to take note of where we are parked in a large parking lot, to notice our surroundings, and to stay grounded. I have been notoriously poor in all of these things. In order to strengthen myself in this area, I took up pottery some years ago, long before I had ever heard of Sandplay. Sandplay was a natural outgrowth of my work with clay as a grounding technique. I still have some minor problems with Sensation, but it is now a much stronger function than it was in the past.

I believe that patients having the same typology as the therapist need special focus and attention because it becomes too easy to fall into the blind spots that we all have, just by virtue of having the same typology. It is often helpful to seek supervision with someone having a different personality type than yourself in order to address these similarities. The converse of this is true as well. For example, when therapists work with a patient having an opposite personality structure than themselves, the need arises to be doubly conscious of the differences in order to best interpret the patient's sand picture. By paying conscious attention to one's own personality typology when analyzing a patient's Sandplay work, a deeper understanding of the dynamics in their constructions is possible. I have found it essential to take a few minutes at the end of each session to consciously attend to this issue. Such an analysis is not discussed with the patient, but may be transmitted nonverbally, thereby enriching the experience for the maker. Kalff believed that an unspoken understanding occurred between the therapist and the maker and that this was a major contributor to the healing process.

The role of the Sandplay therapist, like Sandplay itself, is multifaceted. One needs to be a good observer and listener, attuned to the many verbal and nonverbal nuances that are expressed during the process. One must be able to tolerate mess, accept whatever is presented, never sit in judgment as to the worth of a sand picture. Patients often want to know if the therapist approves or disapproves of the construction, so that great care must be taken to avoid comments that can be misconstrued by the maker. It is the *process* that is the healing factor, not whether the therapist approves. One must have solid training in Sandplay, continually explore whatever may seem to require further study (such as symbols, archetypes, and myths), continually work on one's own issues in some form or other, and have ongoing supervision.

By its very nature, Sandplay is capable of touching the deep, spiritual aspect of the Self and can call up all of the positive and negative aspects of our being. Sandplay and the richness inherent in it is truly "soul work." It is important for anyone who contemplates its use to understand both the potential depths that can be achieved and the possible pitfalls. One learns to honor the process and to protect the maker from moving too swiftly into uncharted territory. There is always the danger that a fragile ego can be overwhelmed when one moves too quickly. Sandplay requires devotion and dedication to the process if it is to be practiced in a responsible, questing way.

The above recommendations are for anyone wanting to practice Sandplay based upon a Jungian framework. Similar recommendations apply, as well, for those who choose to use sandplay from other theoretical bases, such as family systems. The reality is that not everyone wishes to or is able to work in the same way as those who practice from a Jungian orientation. The training requires a significant amount of time and money. This does not mean that it is impossible to use sandplay in other ways, because many therapists are doing so. (When used with a different theoretical base, it is usually referred to as "sand tray work.") What it does mean is that other approaches will not achieve the depths that are possible through a Jungian orientation (although I do understand that others might argue this point). I would like to stress that whatever one uses as a theoretical base, the work must be practiced with all the care and compassion one has at his disposal.

Since this book addresses two different aspects of sandplay, that of the Jungian model for individual therapy and that of family systems, let us turn now to an examination of the person of the therapist when the work is with families.

The qualities of acceptance, nonjudgmentalism, and openness, so vital in Sandplay therapy, are all equally essential when one uses the family systems model. However, one must "change hats" and focus more on the interactional communication patterns that exist between family members than on the archetypal level of one person.

When using a family therapy model, as when using individual Sandplay, it is important for the therapist to have resolved his family of origin issues so that he has no blinders on, or at least as few as possible. If one continues to be afflicted with a mother or father complex, these will, most assuredly, be transmitted to one's patients and affect the outcome of whatever type of therapy is practiced.

In sandplay with families, one is generally more directive in approach than when working with an individual, which is where the creativity of the practitioner is called upon. It becomes possible for the therapist to use any number of interventions from a family systems orientation. For example, one can structure families into two teams in order to address various issues such as scapegoating or parentification, or one can instruct the family to make a picture, nonverbally or verbally, again dependent upon the family dynamics. Another useful technique is to have the family construct a genogram (McGoldrick and Gerson 1985) in the sand, using only animals. A *genogram* is a pictorial record that displays families over three generations (and includes significant dates, such as births, marriages, divorces, deaths of important family members, geographical information, etc.). The miniatures chosen by different family members are particularly enlightening. For example, is Mother depicted as a dragon and Father as a pussy cat? Is a sibling represented by a rat or a dog? The creativity of the therapist can encourage this type of playful communication among family members and can contribute additional understanding of family dynamics that can be incorporated into treatment.

I have alluded to aspects of transference and countertransference dynamics and will add a brief word here. It has been suggested that transference is lessened when one uses Sandplay with individuals because the transference is to the tray rather than to the therapist. I do not concur with this assumption because of my firm belief that it is the person of the therapist that is the healing factor, and that the sand tray is the tool that assists the process. I also believe that attention to countertransference dynamics is essential, which is why I have stressed the need for training and ongoing supervision. Countertransference has usually had a negative connotation attached to it; however, when one is aware of one's countertransferential traps, or blind spots, one can make valuable use of this phenomenon. For example, during a session a therapist might begin to feel uneasy, angry, or anxious for some unknown reason. Often, the reason lies in material the client has presented, which taps into the unconscious of the therapist, causing a visceral reaction. How one chooses to use this information can positively or negatively affect the therapy. Again, I would stress the need for ongoing supervision to help with such issues.

In summary, the therapist who uses sandplay with either individuals or families faces a big challenge. She must be well trained and creative, and needs to have as much self-understanding as possible in order to experiment with a new technique in a responsible way and to tenderly care for all the psyches that are entrusted to her.

⦅❦ 8 ❦⦆

Similarities and Differences

This chapter examines some of the similarities and differences between the two methods of sandplay that have been described in this book: individual Jungian Sandplay therapy with children and family sandplay therapy.

The similarities are somewhat obvious. Both methods use the same equipment: two sand boxes, one containing wet sand and the other dry, and a collection of miniatures. The role of the therapist remains the same, no matter which method is used. He needs to be thoroughly trained in the method employed. Both individual Sandplay and family sandplay require that the therapist continue to grow professionally, to study, to attend training workshops, to have his work supervised, and to continue, as well, to grow through his own personal development. I believe that all of these areas should be pursued as long as one remains in practice. Otherwise we become complacent, and it becomes far too easy for us to fall back into our own blind spots.

The differences in the two methods have been outlined in Chapters One and Two and are summarized below:

The Jungian model is designed solely for treatment of an individual adult or child. The focus is upon helping the person to "individuate," to use Jung's terminology. Individuation is that stage of psychic development that is never fully achieved but can be approximated through psychotherapeutic methods based on the Jungian model. Individual Sandplay therapy (described in Chapter One), requires a thorough grounding in the theories of Jung, combined with the work of Kalff. It also includes Neumann's work related to stages of child development. Familiarity with this material enables the therapist to be a careful observer of the work being produced in the sand. Some understanding of the archetypal level of the psyche, as developed by Jung during his lifetime, is required. I believe that all of this information must be applied in order to achieve an in-depth analysis of what transpires during Sandplay therapy. I also believe that an understanding and use of Jung's theories of personality types is another invaluable aid when one attempts to interpret or analyze a sand production, whether it is the work of an individual or a family.

When the assessment indicates that a case should be treated by family therapy, other criteria are used. Family therapy is often the treatment of choice when one member's symptomatology has impacted directly on all the other members. The focus of family treatment, then, is upon realigning a system that has gone awry. Dynamics such as triangling, scapegoating, parentification, faulty communication patterns, and so on, are the focus of treatment, as well as traumatic situations such as death, divorce, child or spouse neglect or abuse, alcoholism and/or drug addiction. Through family therapy it becomes possible to alleviate the stress of all family members so that each is enabled to resume a healthier relationship with the others. This, in turn, assists the individual members to relate to others outside of the family system in more appropriate ways. When dysfunctional family issues exist, similar problems usually have also arisen outside the family, affecting the member's interactions with others at work or at school. Treatment of the family, then, generalizes outward to improve other relationships.

Traditional Jungian analysis, in an adult, is often begun as a way to accomplish "soul work." The work of soul implies that one is on a conscious spiritual journey for the deeper meaning of one's life. This can be accomplished with Sandplay therapy, although it is more commonly done through a verbal analysis that includes dream work. The child, through a completed process of Sandplay therapy, successfully accomplishes the stage of ego/Self integration, which, broadly speaking, could equate to the "soul work" of the adult. I do not mean to imply that future therapy for a child might be precluded; one has no way of knowing what other life events might occur that would warrant another period of therapy. However, I believe that future therapy can build successfully on what has been accomplished at an earlier stage of development.

There are some individuals who feel that only those practicing from a Kalffian orientation are entitled to use the term Sandplay. I believe that it makes no difference whether one refers to this technique as "Sandplay" or "sand tray"; the process is the same, provided one practices responsibly. I believe, as well, that to term Sandplay "Kalffian" is to ignore the significant contributions of Jung, Lowenfeld, Neumann, and others. Without Jung, there would have been no Kalffian Sandplay, at least not in the way that she developed it. Kalff integrated

Jungian and Lowenfeldian models, then added her own contributions from her study of Zen Buddhism. All of these influences affect the way that one practices Sandplay today. Each therapist builds on the history of any given method and then adds his or her own unique interpretations and understandings to the work.

One cannot forget that one's own personal history also plays a vital part. For example, if a therapist is a child of divorce she might have a natural affinity for working with this population. If one has undergone and resolved a difficult divorce situation as an adult she might be able to work with divorce situations quite well. However, I would urge, as I have throughout this book, that one's personal journey be thoroughly explored in a therapeutic setting, either through individual or family therapy. Before practicing family therapy, it is important for the practitioner to have successfully dealt with her own family-of-origin issues.

When sandplay is added to family therapy, the therapist must realize that she is entering virgin territory and that it is her own creativity that will prove to be the single most effective tool for helping families that are seeking professional guidance. The future of sandplay, whether with a child, adult, or family, lies in the creative energy of each practicing therapist.

Because sandplay therapy is relatively new, it is important for therapists to record and document their work so that others can learn and benefit from it. No single method suits every situation. Our strength lies in experience with a diversity of approaches and it is through diversity that sandplay will live and grow.

◖ Addendum ◗
My Personal Journey

This book is the happy result of many years of struggle and discovery, both personal and professional. My Sandplay journey began in 1980. I was employed at that time by our local mental health center as a senior psychiatric social worker on a children's team. I was also deeply engrossed in my own Jungian analysis and was attending a Jungian group for supervision with another analyst. Because he knew of my interest in working with children, my personal analyst told me about Sandplay during one session that spring. I was immediately excited by the idea and decided that I had to explore it further. He suggested that I travel to Switzerland to meet Frau Kalff, and that I go to California to see Edith Sullwold and Kay Bradway. That day I went to the New York Jung Library and took out Dora Kalff's (1971) book, *Sandplay: Mirror of a Child's Psyche*. A flyer was on the counter for a workshop to be offered that summer by the University of California Extension Division, at Santa Cruz. Kalff and Sullwold were among those listed as speakers. The conference was entitled "Jung and Education." As it happened, my Jungian group supervisory meeting was held that evening. The supervisor handed out the very same flyer I had picked up earlier that day, calling attention to it for those of us who were working with children. I could not avoid the synchronistic implications. My mind was immediately made up and I proceeded to plan for the trip to Switzerland.

My first step was to request a leave of absence over the summer. I did not want to take just the two weeks of the conference as my vacation and then go directly back to work. I felt intuitively that I would need time to integrate the experience. My request was denied, so I resigned. A very rash move, one might say, yet one that I have never regretted.

The lectures by Dora Kalff fulfilled my highest expectations. It was much more than the material covered. It was her presence, her ease, her accessibility, her being, her soul that came through with every word that she spoke. Her English was impeccable and I marveled at her communication skills. The lectures were held in an upstairs living room in her home, which offered a very warm, welcoming area away from the stiffness of the lectures in the Jung Institute. Dora's dog (I've forgotten his name), was always part of the gathering.[1] All of the participants in the conference were scheduled to go to her home

---

1. After Frau Kalff's death, her son Martin offered a Sandplay Conference which I attended in 1992. It was held in the Kalff home, the first one to be led by Martin, who is now carrying on her work. During the final dinner of the conference, Martin and his wife arrived quite late. We all thought that was quite odd, and only learned the next day that their tardiness was due to the dog's death. He had been struck by a car just as the Kalffs were about to leave home that evening. It felt synchronistic to me that the dog had welcomed me to that first workshop with Frau Kalff and was again there to welcome me on Martin's first. It was as if the dog had completed his tenure and now turned the proceedings over to the next generation.

on two separate days. I was completely hooked after the first. As we were leaving, I told one new friend how very much I wanted to have some individual time with Frau Kalff to experience this remarkable medium (and person) for myself. She suggested that I hurry to approach her with my request, as many others from our group were doing the same thing. I took the advice and was able to arrange an individual session—in fact, two—during the time that we were there.

The Kalff home itself was a most remarkable place. It was a fourteenth-century farm house, which Frau Kalff told us was built over an ancient temple. An adjoining house had been converted into a Zen retreat. The Dalai Lama was a guest there several times when he visited Switzerland.

Art therapy was held twice a week in a downstairs area in the Zen building. These sessions were almost as intense as the Sandplay experience. The entire ambiance connected to those two weeks intimately engaged the deepest parts of me.

The Sandplay room was the most fascinating place imaginable. There were unique and precious items of every description. I felt like Alice in Wonderland. Frau Kalff was my grandmother reincarnated. She struck many of the attendees as a personification of the Great Mother archetype.

My first session with Dora Kalff fulfilled all of my expectations and brought up many new ones. First, her minimal observations of what I had produced showed a deep insight into my personal struggle. Most important of all, however, was my visceral reaction to the experience. I was struck by the power, the numinosity, the relief at being able to find a new way of expressing the seemingly inexpressible. How much of that was related to the material and how much to Dora Kalff's presence, I really do not know. I just know that it was a turning point in my life and that she became my ego ideal, my role model for what I hoped to achieve. I was overjoyed that I had made the decision to resign my post at home.

The weekend between the two lectures by Dora Kalff had been planned as trips to local sites that were meaningful to Jung (and Jungians). The first day of the weekend dawned dark and rainy, as the entire preceding week had been. We donned our raincoats and toted our umbrellas as we boarded the bus that was to take us to Bollingen, Jung's summer retreat, and then on to Einsiedeln for Vespers. This was to be followed by a dinner at the home of John Hill and his wife. Dr. Hill was another of our gifted lecturers, his specialty being Celtic mythology.

Louise Mahdi was in charge of our bus that weekend, and she read sections of Jung's (1965) autobiography, *Memories, Dreams, Reflections,* to us on the road to Bollingen. A Swiss guide was also on the bus. He acted as interpreter between our group and the bus driver, who spoke no English. We were told that we would not be able to enter the Bollingen property because members of the Jung family were living there and their privacy needed to be respected, so we parked about a mile from the property and walked back through the pouring rain to peek through the fence at this revered place. While we stood in awe, staring but not able to really see much, our Swiss guide proceeded through the gate. He had never heard of Jung and didn't have the sense of awe and propriety that we all had. Several minutes later he reappeared and waved for us to pass through the gate. We were invited in! About half of us entered; the rest went back to the bus. I still remember the wonderment, the beauty, the sense of deep connectedness that permeated the atmosphere as we respectfully circled around the outside walls of Bollingen. We saw Jung's carvings on the stone (which have been well-described in *Memories, Dreams, Reflections*) and on the house and the beautiful outdoor cooking area that was adorned with bouquets of flowers, even in the pouring rain. Such magic!

On the way back to the bus, we knew we would be reprimanded for what we had done but, like all children, we felt the experience was worth the punishment. We decided not to gloat or say too much to the others; we did not want to give rise to any animosity from our peers. Instead, what we wanted most was to hold the experience deep within ourselves. Louise was less than pleased with us, but managed to withhold many comments. Nevertheless, her displeasure was definitely felt! I suppose, had I been in her place, I might have been annoyed as well, but that offer had simply been too much to resist.

The Cathedral at Einsiedeln was the next site that we visited. I was unprepared for this as well. I am not Catholic and was unfamiliar with the protocol. Our visit was scheduled for 4:00 P.M., to coincide with Vespers. The church was one of the most immense ones that I had ever seen. Smells of incense mingled with the dampness of the atmosphere. Organ music filled every space with sonorous tones that I felt deep within my body. I felt a soul revival like nothing I had ever experienced before. The closing moments of the ceremony were the most powerful of all. All of the priests, perhaps fifty or sixty, proceeded to an alcove near the front door and sang the Salve Regina. Until then, I had failed to see the Black Madonna, nor had I known of her existence. The power of that moment is etched in my mind. Since then, I have read everything I could find about this figure. One source that I found quite moving is in Marion Woodman's (1985) book, *The Pregnant Virgin: A*

Process of Psychological Transformation.[2] She was standing in her own special niche, shining in all her glory, holding a black infant. My friends and I stood transfixed, holding hands, as tears streamed down our faces. The pageantry of so many centuries of worship sank deep into my Protestant soul. I could almost have converted at that moment. I knew, deep within, that this was probably the most powerful experience of my life, but I could not explain why. I still cannot. I knew that I would return, and with the hope that someday I might learn what the significance of all of this was for me. I have returned numerous times. Each time I go back it is like going home. The Black Madonna with all her mystery, as I know her now, is the epitome of grace and soul. I also know that she speaks to everyone, irrespective of each person's religious belief.

This is not quite the end of my story. The next day, another dark and rainy one, the class attended art therapy, which was held in a downstairs area of the Jung Institute. I do not recall what the assignment was. I only recall that my tears began to drop, one by one, on the page. They kept coming faster and faster. I went to the ladies room in an attempt to pull myself together. I could not. I finally went out and sat in the boat house, which is on the lake. I sobbed and sobbed and sobbed some

---

2. The history of the Black Madonna of Einsiedeln reveals that she has been a healing site for pilgrimages for many centuries. The reason she is black, as local legend tells it, is because of the centuries of votive candles that were burned at her feet and turned her skin and that of the child she held, black. Others have said that she was hidden in caves during wars and turned black in the process. Her black color, according to some Jungian interpretations, is because she represents the deepest possible soul image for the modern woman, as well as a Great Mother archetype.

more. I looked for Louise Mahdi but she was not there that morning. The sun finally made an appearance and I looked out at the scene and felt lonelier than I had felt in many years. I desperately wanted either my mother, who had been dead for a long time, or else my analyst, who was in New York.

After some time had passed, John Allan, another of the group leaders, came to me and said, "Lois, we have a very nice woman from California who has offered to spend as much time with you as you need. Do you want to talk to her?" Of course I did and when she arrived, she was my mother and my analyst all rolled into one. Edith Sullwold became another powerful role model for me and one of the many people I need to thank for being influential in the journey that has culminated in this book.

My journey has been meaningful and yet arduous, and I would not change any of it even if I could. I have learned more than I ever thought possible. I would just like to end with sincere, heartfelt thanks to all of my fellow journeyers and to the many organizations that have invited me to present my work. I offer a special thank you to the numerous persons who have come to me for help with their journeys and who have taught me so much.

I will close with a message that was sent to me recently by the mother of a girl (who wrote it) now 11 years old, whom I treated seven or eight years ago—a message that, alone, would make the journey all worthwhile.

A Special Helper and Friend
by SW

After my dad died, I was very sorrowful. My mom took me to a special Sand Play Therapist for kids and this helped me to learn to cope with his death.

My dad died of cancer when I was three years old. It was very sad! I was just devastated and confused.

My mom took me to a psychologist that practices Sand Play Therapy. Her name is Lois Carey and her husband's name is David Carey. My dad's name was David too. David Carey is a musician. Since Lois works at home, when I went there, I sometimes got to hear music.

Lois has a room with a sand box of wet sand and a sand box of dry sand. When I went there, I played in the sand and made a scene with my choice of little figures and props. She took pictures of my scene, and I told a story about my scene that explains feelings. Sometimes I went into the office-type room, and played games, colored, or just talked and told stories.

After my dad died, I started going to Lois. I had fun with Lois and she took my mind off my dad and convinced me that everything would be okay! She made me feel a lot better and helped me to understand what was going on and what had happened!

Death is very difficult for a little kid to understand. I am glad that there are special people like Lois to help you get through it.

ᗏ Appendix ᗓ

Sample Permission Form
and Suggested Miniatures
and Sources

SAMPLE PERMISSION FORM

My signature below will grant permission to LOIS CAREY, M.S.W., A.C.S.W., B.C.D., to use the slides of my child's or my sand pictures for training workshops for professional groups and/or to illustrate any future articles or books authored by her. The child's name (or mine) is _____ and the birthdate is _____. It is my understanding that there will be no identifying features such as actual names, dates, location, or photos that show the child's face, etc., relevant to the maker of the sand pictures, but that the information will be presented in a disguised form as is generally approved in the professional literature.

Print Name _____

Signature _____

Address _____

_____

SUGGESTED MINIATURES AND SOURCES

Materials in General Use

A. *LIVING CREATURES*—in sufficient numbers to portray large scenes
    People—men, women, children—various occupations, royalty, historic, farming, Indians, soldiers, knights
    Non-Human—animals: domestic, wild, prehistoric; sea creatures, birds, fish, butterflies

B. *FANTASY FIGURES*—Disney, superheroes, fairies, mermaids, etc.

C. *SCENERY*—buildings (all types), vegetation (trees, flowers), bridges, fences

D. *TRANSPORTATION*
    Land—cars, fire trucks, ambulance, police cars
    Sea—boats, ships
    Air—planes, helicopters, military

E. *EQUIPMENT*—implements for roads and farms, signs, children's playground, hospital beds, doctor kits

F. *MISCELLANEOUS*—wishing well, coffin, rocks, shells, beads

Sandplay Supplies and Accessories

BIJOUX ARCHETYPES
P.O. Box 4525
Walnut Creek, CA 94596
(510) 939-3111

DREAMTIME MINIATURES
1707 S.E. 33rd St.
Portland, OR 97214
(503) 234-0431

PLAYROOMS
P.O. Box 2660
Petaluma, CA 94953
(800) 667-2470

SELF-ESTEEM SHOP
4607 N. Woodward
Royal Oak, MI 48073
(800) 251-8336

OAK HILL SPECIALTIES
P.O. Box 152
Cloverdale, CA 95425
(800) 615-4155

ROSE TRAVEL KITS
102 Foster Ranch Road
Trinidad, TX 75163
(800) 713-2252

Also flea markets, garage sales, toy stores, etc.

☙ References ☙

Ackerman, N. (1970). Child participation in family therapy. *Family Process* 9:403–410.

Author Unknown. (1991). Bringing up baby: family therapy rediscovers its youngest clients. *Family Therapy Networker*, July/Aug, pp. 1–8.

Axline, V. (1947). *Play Therapy.* New York: Ballantine.

Bow, J. (1993). Overcoming resistance. In *The Therapeutic Powers of Play*, ed. C. Schaefer, pp. 17–40. Northvale, NJ: Jason Aronson.

Bowen, M. (1978). *Family Therapy in Clinical Practice.* New York: Jason Aronson.

Bowyer, L. (1970). *The Lowenfeld World Technique.* Oxford: Pergamon.

Brody, V. (1993). *The Dialogue of Touch.* Treasure Island, FL: Developmental Play Training.

Buhler, C. (1951a). The World Test: a projective technique. *Journal of Child Psychiatry* 2:4–23.

——— (1951b). The World Test: manual of directions. *Journal of Child Psychiatry* 2:69–81.

——— (1952). National differences in World Test projective patterns. *Journal of Projective Techniques* 16(1):42–55.

Buhler, C., and Kelly, G. (1941). *The World Test: A Measurement of Emotional Disturbance.* New York: Psychological Corporation.

Caplan, F., and Caplan, T. (1974). *The Power of Play.* New York: Anchor Books.

Carey, L. (1991). Family sandplay therapy. *Arts in Psychotherapy* 18:231–239.

Cirlot, J. (1962). *A Dictionary of Symbols*. New York: Philosophical Library.

DeDomenico, G. (1988). *Sand Tray, World Play: A Comprehensive Guide to the Use of the Sand Tray in Psychotherapeutic and Transformational Settings*. Self-published.

Des Lauriers, A. (1962). *The Experience of Reality in Childhood Schizophrenia*. New York: International Universities Press.

Diagnostic and Statistical Manual of Mental Disorders (1994). 4th ed. Washington, DC: American Psychiatric Association.

Edinger, E. (1972). *Ego and Archetype*. New York: Penguin.

Eichoff, L. (1952). Dreams in sand. *British Journal of Psychiatry* 98:235–243.

Fischer, L. (1950). A new psychological tool in function: preliminary clinical experience with the Bolgar-Fischer world test. *American Journal of Orthopsychiatry* 20:281–292.

Freud, A. (1946). *The Psychoanalytical Treatment of Children*. London: Imago.

Gil, E. (1994). *Play in Family Therapy*. New York: Guilford.

Guerney, B. (1964). Filial therapy: description and rationale. *Journal of Consulting Psychology* 28:303–310, 450–460.

Guerney, B., Guerney, L., and Andronico, M. (1966). Filial therapy. *Yale Scientific Magazine* 40:6–14, 20.

Gurman, A., Kniskern, D., and Pinsolf, W. (1985). Research on the process and outcome of family therapy. In *Handbook of Psychotherapy and Behavior Change*, 3rd ed., ed. S. Garfield and A. Bergin, pp. 525–623. New York: Wiley.

Homberger, E. (a.k.a. Erik Erikson) (1937). Dramatic productions test. In *Explorations in Personality*, ed. H. A. Murray, pp. 552–582. New York: Oxford University Press.

Jernberg, A. (1989). *Theraplay: A New Treatment Using Structured*

Play for Problem Children and Their Families. San Francisco: Jossey-Bass.

Jung, C. (1956). Symbols of transformation. In *Collected Works*, Vol. 5. Princeton, NJ: Bollingen Paperback.

———— (1959). The psychology of the child archetype. *Collected Works*, Vol. 9 (1):151–181. Princeton: Princeton University Press.

———— (1965). *Memories, Dreams, Reflections*. New York: Vintage.

———— (1976). Psychological types. *Collected Works*, Vol. 6, 2nd ed. Princeton: Princeton/Bollingen Paperback.

———— (1980). The archetypes and the collective unconscious. *Collected Works*, Vol. 9, part 1. Princeton: Bollingen Paperback.

Kalff, D. (1966). The archetype as a healing factor. *Psychologia* 9:177–184.

———— (1971). *Sandplay: Mirror of a Child's Psyche*. San Francisco: Browser.

———— (1980). *Sandplay*, 2nd ed. Santa Monica, CA: Sigo Press.

———— (1981). Foreword. In *Sandplay Studies: Origins, Theory and Practice*, by K. Bradway et al., pp. vii–ix. San Francisco: C. G. Jung Institute.

Keith, D., and Whitaker, C. (1981). Play therapy: a paradigm for work with families. *Journal of Marital and Family Therapy* 7:243–254.

Klein, M. (1959). *The Psychoanalysis of Children*, 3rd ed. London: Hogarth.

Kwiatkowska, H. (1978). *Family Therapy and Evaluation Through Art*. Springfield, IL: Charles C Thomas.

Landgarten, H. (1987). *Family Art Psychotherapy: A Clinical Guide and Casebook*. New York: Brunner/Mazel.

Landreth, G. (1991). *Play Therapy: The Art of the Relationship*. Muncie, IN: Accelerated Development.

Landreth, G., Homeyer, L., Glover, G., and Sweeney, D. (1996). *Play Therapy Interventions with Children's Problems*. Northvale, NJ: Jason Aronson.

Lowenfeld, M. (1979). *The World Technique*. London: Allen & Unwin.

Mayer, A. (1983). *Incest: A Treatment Manual for Therapy with Victims, Spouses and Offenders*. Holmes Beach, FL: Learning Publications.

McGoldrick, M., and Gerson, R. (1985). *Genograms in Family Assessment*. New York: Norton.

Miller, W. (1994). Family play therapy: history, theory, and convergence. In *Family Play Therapy*, ed. C. S. Schaefer and L. Carey, pp. 3–19. Northvale, NJ: Jason Aronson.

Mitchell, R., and Friedman, H. (1994). *Sandplay: Past, Present and Future*. London and New York: Routledge.

Moustakas, C. (1953). *Children in Play Therapy*. New York: McGraw-Hill.

——— (1973). *The Child's Discovery of Himself*. New York: Jason Aronson.

——— (1975). *Who Will Listen? Children and Parents in Therapy*. New York: Ballantine.

——— (1981). *Rhythms, Rituals, and Relationships*. Detroit, MI: Center for Humanistic Studies.

Myers-Briggs, I. (1962). *The Myers-Briggs Type Indicator*. Palo Alto, CA: Consulting Psychologists Press.

Neumann, E. (1954). *The Origins and History of Consciousness*. Princeton: Bollingen Series.

——— (1955). *The Great Mother: An Analysis of the Archetype*. Princeton: Bollingen Series.

——— (1973). *The Child*. Boston: Shambhala.

Nichols, W., and Everett, C. (1986). *Systemic Family Therapy*. New York: Guilford.

Oaklander, V. (1978). *Windows to Our Children: A Gestalt Therapy Approach to Our Children and Adolescents*. Highland, NY: Gestalt Journal Press.

Orgun, I. (1973). Playroom setting for diagnostic family interviews. *American Journal of Psychiatry* 130(5):540–542.

Parke, H. (1977). *Festivals of the Athenians*. New York: Cornell University Press.

Piercy, F. P., Sprenkle, D. H., Wetchler, J., and Associates. (1996). Structural, strategic, and systemic family therapies. In *Family Therapy Sourcebook*, 2nd ed., pp. 50–78. New York: Guilford.

Satir, V. (1964). *Conjoint Family Therapy*. Palo Alto, CA: Science and Behavior Books.

Schaefer, C. (1994). Play therapy for psychic trauma in children. In *Handbook of Play Therapy*, vol. 2, ed. K. O'Connor and C. Schaefer. New York: Wiley.

Schaefer, C., and Carey, L., eds. (1994). *Family Play Therapy*. Northvale, NJ: Jason Aronson.

Scharff, D., and Scharff, J. (1987). *Object Relations Family Therapy*. Northvale, NJ: Jason Aronson.

Scharff, J. (1989). Play with young children in family therapy. In *Children in Family Therapy: Treatment and Training*, pp. 159–172. New York: Haworth.

Siegelman, E. (1990). *Metaphor and Meaning in Psychotherapy*. New York: Guilford.

Siever, R. (1988). *Sand*. New York: W. H. Freeman.

Sjolund, M. (1981) Play-diagnosis and therapy in Sweden: the Erica-method. *Journal of Clinical Psychology* 37(2):322–325.

Spare, G. (1990). Are there any rules? (musings of a peripatetic sandplayer). In *Sandplay Studies: Origins, Theory and Practice*, by K. Bradway et al., pp. 195–208. Boston, MA: Sigo.

Stevens, A. (1982). *Archetypes*. New York: Quill.

Sweeney, D. (1997). *Counseling Children Through the World of Play*. Wheaton, IL: Tyndale House.

von Bertalanffy, L. (1962). *General System Theory*. New York: George Braziller.

Wachtel, E. (1992). An integrative approach to working with troubled children and their families. *Journal of Psychotherapy Integration* (2,3):207–224.

Webb, N., ed. (1993). *Helping Bereaved Children: A Handbook for Practitioners*. New York: Guilford.

Weinrib, E. (1983). *Images of the Self*. Boston: Sigo.

Wilmer, H. (1991). *Practical Jung*. Wilmette, IL: Chiron.

Woodman, M. (1985). *The Pregnant Virgin: A Process of Psychological Transformation*. Toronto: Inner City Books.

―――― (1993). *Conscious Femininity: Interviews with Marion Woodman*. Toronto: Inner City Books.

Zilbach, J. (1989). The family life cycle: a framework for understanding children in family therapy. In *Children in Family Contexts: Perspectives on Treatment*, ed. L. Combrinck-Graham, pp. 46–66. New York: Guilford.

⟨⟨ Credits ⟩⟩

☙ Index ❧

Abreaction, sandplay, xviii
Accessories, resources for, 189
Ackerman, N., xv, 41, 42, 51
Adjustment reactions, diagnostic examples, 96–98
Age level, sandplay treatment, 72
Aggressive world signs, sandplay, 7
Anima, Jungian psychology, 16
Animal/vegetative step, Neumann and, 23
Animus, Jungian psychology, 16–17
Anxiety, diagnostic examples, 92–94
Archetypes, sandplay, 11–20
Association for Play Therapy (APT), 29, 32
Attention Deficit Hyperactivity Disorder child-centered family sandplay therapy, 118

family sandplay therapy example, 137–138
Axline, V., 35, 37

Bateson, G., 42
Behaviorism, play therapy methods, 33–34
Birthmark, diagnostic examples, 110–111
Boundaries, sandplay, xix–xx
Bow, J., xix
Bowen, M., 45
Bowyer, L. R., 9
Bowyer, R., 6
Bradley, K., 177
Bradway, K., 28
Brody, V., 34
Buhler, C., 6, 7

Caplan, F., xii
Caplan, T., xii
Carey, L., 49, 54, 56
Chagall, M., 5
Chaos, Neumann and, 23

Child-centered family sandplay therapy, example of, 115–136
Child-centered play therapy, methods, 35–36, 50–52
Children, communication requirements, ix–x
Cirlot, J., 119, 124
Collective, Neumann and, 24
Communication
 requirements for, ix–x
 sandplay, xxii
 sandplay and, xiv–xv
Communicationist family therapy, models, 43–44
Communication theory, strate-gic family therapy, 42
Complexes, Jungian psychology, 14
Conduct Disorder, family sandplay therapy, 137
Confidentiality, sandplay treatment, 69, 71
Control, sandplay, xxiii–xxiv
Crisis, family sandplay therapy, 114–115

DeDomenico, G., 29, 59
Defenses, sandplay, xxiii
Depression, diagnostic examples, 94–96
Des Lauriers, A., 34

Diagnostic and Statistical Manual of Mental Disorders (DSM-IV), x, 78, 117, 137
Diagnostic examples, 91–111
 adjustment reactions, 96–98
 anxiety, 92–94
 birthmark, 110–111
 depression, 94–96
 divorce, 91–92
 learning disabilities, 101–106
 oppositional disorder, 106–107
 sandplay, 91–111. *See also* Diagnostic examples
 sexual abuse, 99–100
 speech problems, 109
 visual impairment, 108
Dissociative Identity Disorder, child-centered family sandplay therapy, 117
Distorted world signs, sandplay, 8–10
Divorce, diagnostic examples, 91–92

Edinger, E., 26–27
Ego/Self
 Edinger and, 26–27
 Jungian psychology, 17–19
 Neumann and, 23–24
Eichoff, L., xii
Emotion, nonverbal, sandplay, xvi–xvii

Empty world signs, sandplay, 7–8
Equipment, of sandplay office, 57–66
Erica Method, 9–10
Erikson, E. H., 4, 25–26
Erikson, M., 44
Everett, C., 40, 41, 42, 46, 47, 52

Family sandplay therapy, 113–161
child-centered example, 115–136
comparisons, 173–176
family crisis example, 136–160
outcomes, 160–161
overview, 113–115
Family therapy, 38–56. *See also* Family sandplay therapy; Play therapy; Sandplay
children in, 38–39
historical perspective on, 39–40
Jungian sandplay and, xxvii–xxviii
models of, 41–47
communicationist, 43–44
psychodynamic, 41–42
strategic, 42
structural, 43
systemic, 44–47

play therapy and, 48–53
premises of, 47–48
sandplay and, xv, xix, 53–56
Fighting step, Neumann and, 23
Filial therapy, play therapy methods, 33, 50
Fischer, L., 6
Freud, A., 25, 38
Freud, S., 10, 12, 31
Friedman, H., 4, 25

General Systems Theory, 44
Gestalt play therapy, methods, 36, 50
Gil, E., xv
Great Mother, Jungian psychology, 14, 22
Guerney, B., 33, 50
Guerney, L., 33
Gurman, A., 40

Haley, J., 42, 44
Harding, G., 9
Hero, Jungian psychology, 15–16
Holding capacity, family play therapy, 50–51

Incest. *See* Sexual abuse
Individuation, 13
Inner Child, Jungian psychology, 17
International Society of Sandplay Therapists (ISST), 28

Interpersonal relationships,
  sandplay, xiii–xiv
Intrapsychic issues, sandplay,
  xxiv
I–Thou concept, 24

Jackson, D., 42, 44
Jernberg, A., 34
Jung, C. G., 2, 10–20, 166,
  167, 174, 180
Jung, E., 20
Jungian sandplay, family
  therapy and, xxvii–xxviii.
  See Sandplay

Kalff, D., xii, xiii, xiv, xxi, 2,
  4, 10, 18, 20–21, 22,
  28, 58, 59, 63, 174,
  175, 177, 178, 179,
  180
Kalff, M., 28, 166, 178n1
Keith, D., xix, 50, 51
Kelly, G., 7
Kinesthetic quality, sandplay,
  xvii
Klein, M., 37–38
Kwiatkowska, H., xv

Landgarten, H., 55
Landreth, G., ix, xiii, 35, 36,
  42
Learning disabilities,
  diagnostic examples,
  101–106
Limits, sandplay, xix–xx

Lowenfeld, M., xxiv, 2, 3–10,
  11, 20, 38

Madanes, C., 42
Mahdi, L., 180, 183
Mayer, A., 117
Metaphor, therapeutic,
  sandplay, xx–xxi
Miller, W., 48
Miniatures, sources of, 188
Minuchin, S., 43
Mitchell, R. R., 4, 6, 25
Montalvo, C., 44
Mother role, child-centered
  family sandplay therapy,
  117
Moustakas, C., 36
Myers-Briggs Inventory, 167

Navajo Indians, 3
Negative transference, child-
  centered family sandplay
  therapy, 122
Neumann, E., 14, 22–25, 88,
  174
Nichols, W., 40, 41, 42, 46,
  47, 52
Nonverbal emotion,
  sandplay, xvi–xvii

Oaklander, V., 50
Object relations play
  therapy, methods, 36,
  50
O'Connor, K., 32

Office, sandplay office,
equipment of, 57–66
Oppositional Disorder
diagnostic examples, 106–
107
family sandplay therapy, 137
Orgun, I., 39

Parentified child concept, 46
Parents
play therapy methods, 36–37
sandplay therapist and,
167–168
sandplay treatment, 69–70
Parke, H., 81
Permission form, sample of,
187
Photography, sandplay office
equipment, 63–64
Piercy, F. P., 40, 42, 43
Play
as communication, ix–x
therapy and, xii–xv
Play therapy, 31–38. *See also*
Family sandplay therapy;
Family therapy; Sandplay
current, 32
defined, xiii
family therapy and, 48–53
history of, 31–32
methods of, 33–37
behaviorism, 33–34
child-centered, 35–36
filial therapy, 33
Theraplay, 34–35

pioneers of, 37–38
sandplay and, xv
Polaroid photography,
sandplay office
equipment, 63–64
Positive transference, child-
centered family sandplay
therapy, 125
Post-traumatic stress disorder,
78
Psychoanalytic play therapy,
methods, 36, 50
Psychodynamic family
therapy, models, 41–42
Psychological Types, Jungian
psychology, 19–20

Release forms, photography,
sandplay office
equipment, 64
Resistance, sandplay, xxi–xxii
Rogers, C., 35, 37

Safety, sandplay treatment,
71–72
Sand, as medium, xi–xii
Sandplay. *See also* Family
sandplay therapy; Family
therapy; Play therapy
benefits and rationale for,
xvi–xxv
case example, 75–91
communication and, xiv–xv
comparisons, 173–176
current status, 28–30

Sandplay (*continued*)
  diagnostic examples, 91–111
  Edinger and, 26–27
  Erikson and, 25–26
  family therapy and, xv, xix,
    53–56
  interpersonal relationships,
    xiii–xiv
  Jung and, 10–20
  Kalff and, 20–21
  Lowenfeld and, 3–10
  miniatures and sources, 188
  Neumann and, 22–25
  overview, 1–2
  supplies and accessories, 188
  trauma and, x–xi
  treatment initiation, 67–74
  treatment structure, 73–74
Sandplay office, equipment
    of, 57–66
Sandplay therapist
  depth psychology, 165–166
  Jungian psychology, 166–
    167
  parents and, 167–168
  personality of, 167
  personal perspective of,
    177–184
  role of, xiv, 168–171
  theoretical orientations, 2
  training of, 163–164
Sandplay Therapists of
    America (STA), 28
Satir, V., 44
Scapegoated child concept, 46

Schaefer, C., xviii, 32, 49
Scharff, D., 50
Scharff, J., 50
Seitz, G., 4
Senex, Jungian psychology,
    15
Sensory base, of trauma, x–xi
Sexual abuse
  child-centered family
    sandplay therapy, 135–
    136
  diagnostic examples, 99–
    100
Sexual identity, family play
    therapy, 51–52
Siegelman, E., xiv, xx
Siever, R., xii
Sjolund, M., 9
Skinner, B. F., 33
Spare, G., xxv
Speech problems, diagnostic
    examples, 109
Sprenkle, D. H., 40
Strategic family therapy,
    models, 42
Structural family therapy,
    models, 43
Sullwold, E., 177
Supplies, resources for, 189
Sweeney, D., x, xix
Systemic family therapy,
    models, 44–47

Terrible Mother, Jungian
    psychology, 14–15

Therapeutic distance,
    sandplay, xvii–xviii
Therapeutic metaphor,
    sandplay, xx–xxi
Therapist. *See* Sandplay
    therapist
Theraplay, play therapy
    methods, 34–35
Therapy, play and, xii–xv
Toy World Test, 6
Transference
    negative, child-centered
        family sandplay
        therapy, 122
    positive, child-centered
        family sandplay
        therapy, 125
    sandplay, xxiv
Trauma
    abreaction, sandplay, xviii
    child-centered family
        sandplay therapy, 119–
        120, 135–136
    communication and, x
    control, sandplay, xxiii–xxiv
    sandplay and, x–xi
    sensory base of, x–xi

Trickster, Jungian psychology,
    16

Verbalization, sandplay, xxiii
Verbal skills, sandplay, xxii
Visual impairment, diagnostic
    examples, 108
von Bertalanffy, L., 44

Wachtel, E., 50
Watzlawick, P., 42
Weakland, J., 44
Webb, N. B., 76
Weinrib, E., xxiv, 3, 18, 21, 28
Wetchler, J. L., 40, 42, 43
Whitaker, C., xix, 50, 51
Wilmer, H., 12, 15
Wise Old Man, Jungian
    psychology, 15
Woodman, M., 12, 181
World Technique, 3, 6, 11,
    20
World Test, 6
Wynne, L., 41

Zen Buddhism, 21, 176
Zilbach, J., 51